# SLAUGHTER OF THE INNOCENTS

# BY THE SAME AUTHOR

# SLAUGHTER OF THE INNOCENTS

*Abortion, Birth Control and Divorce
in Light of Science, Law and Theology*

John Warwick Montgomery

CROSSWAY BOOKS
Westchester, Illinois 60153

141852

All biblical quotations are from the King James Version of the Bible.

*Slaughter of the Innocents: Abortion, Birth Control and Divorce in Light of Science, Law and Theology*
Copyright © 1981 by John Warwick Montgomery. Published by Crossway Books, a division of Good News Publishers, 9825 West Roosevelt Road, Westchester, Illinois 60153.

First printing, 1981
Second printing, 1981

Printed in the United States of America.

Library of Congress Catalog Card Number 81-65469

ISBN 0-89107-216-0

*For*

*my parents,*

*Maurice Warwick and Harriet Smith Montgomery,*

*whose unmerited love for me*

*has never faltered*

*from the moment of my conception*

# CONTENTS

# SLAUGHTER OF THE INNOCENTS

Recall that the young Mary was pregnant under circumstances that today routinely terminate in abortion. In the important theological context of Christmas, the killing of an unborn child is a symbolic killing of the Christchild.

Paul C. Vitz

*Psychology as Religion* (1977), p. 89

# PREFACE

One of the most terrifying passages in the Bible is found embedded in the familiar account of our Lord's nativity. We are told that

Herod, when he saw that he was mocked of the wise men, was exceeding wroth, and sent forth, and slew all the children that were in Bethlehem, and in all the coasts thereof, from two years old and under, according to the time which he had diligently inquired of the wise men. Then was fulfilled that which was spoken by Jeremy the prophet, saying, In Rama was there a voice heard, lamentation, and weeping, and great mourning, Rachel weeping for her children, and would not be comforted, because they are not. But when Herod was dead, behold, an angel of the Lord appeareth in a dream to Joseph in Egypt, saying,

11

Arise, and take the young child and his mother, and go into the land of Israel: for they are dead which sought the young child's life.[1]

This "slaughter of the innocents" was swiftly followed by the death of Herod, the perpetrator of the monstrous deed. God's judgment on the killing of little children is particularly evident from the value the Christmas story places on babyhood and fetal life. Not only is our Lord worshiped while a mere newborn infant, but

when Elisabeth heard the salutation of Mary, the babe [John the Baptist] leaped in her womb; and Elisabeth was filled with the Holy Ghost: and she spake out with a loud voice, and said, Blessed art thou among women, and blessed is the fruit of thy womb. And whence is this to me, that the mother of my Lord should come to me? For, lo, as soon as the voice of thy salutation sounded in mine ears, the babe leaped in my womb for joy.[2]

The essays comprising this volume are predicated on the belief that current abortion practice in the United States is indeed a slaughter of innocents, and that the God of Scripture would have us return to that respect for fetal life which he himself manifested in the giving of his own Son for our salvation. Scientifically, the genetic argument for human personhood commencing at the moment of conception is irrefutable. Jurisprudentially, we can only second the position taken by constitutionalist Joseph P. Witherspoon, the Thomas Shelton Maxey Professor of Law at the University of Texas School of Law, in a symposium in which I myself participated:

*Wade* and *Bolton* are the most erroneous and tragic decisions in the history of constitutional adjudication. They are the most erroneous be-

[1] Matthew 2:16-20.
[2] Luke 1:41-44.

cause the Court openly abandoned its universally acknowledged duty to respect the actual purpose of the framers of a constitutional provision in administering it. That purpose was everywhere manifest in the legislative history leading to the submission and adoption of the Thirteenth and Fourteenth Amendments. That purpose was to reestablish that all human beings, including unborn human children, are persons protected by the Constitution and that no court or other agency of government could define them out of that protection ever again. *Wade* and *Bolton* are also the most tragic decisions in the history of constitutional adjudication because the Court in abandoning its duty under the rule of law or justice under law in human society provides constitutional protection and approval for the deliberate killing of millions of unborn human beings under a constitutional Amendment that guarantees fundamental justice and equal protection under the law to all human beings. These decisions are thus essentially unjust.[3]

George F. Will, in reviewing Woodward and Armstrong's exposé of the Burger Court, declares what is now public knowledge, not mere suspicion:

"The Brethren" confirms what a reading of the Burger Court's chaotic abortion opinion suggested: the result of that case was never in doubt, and nothing but the result—certainly not a grounding of the decision in constitutional law—was important to a majority of the Justices. What began as an assertion of a doctor's right to discretion ended as an assertion of a woman's right to privacy, but it never was going to be more than pure assertion, an act of essentially legislative power. The majority believed that liberalized abortion is *right* and *good*, and that the political system (read: representative government) is *slow*.

The book is a catalog of result-oriented behavior. Such behavior continues.[4]

---

[3]J. P. Witherspoon, "Impact of the Abortion Decisions upon the Father's Role," *The Jurist*, Winter 1975, p. 47. For my contributions to this Symposium, see chapter 2.

[4]George F. Will, *Newsweek*, December 10, 1979, p. 140.

In sum: whether one shines the legal, the medical, or the theological spotlight on current American abortion practice, it illuminates a stark, unprincipled field of blood.

But the innocents are also slaughtered by bad marriages and broken homes. Several of the essays in the present book aim to achieve a more scriptural and responsible view of marriage and divorce, so that the child who escapes the abortionist's knife will be less likely to suffer from a lethal family or parental environment. As a practicing attorney faced almost daily with the wreckage of marriages—many of them Christian marriages—I firmly believe that prevention is overwhelmingly superior to cure.

May the God who analogized marriage to the relation subsisting in eternity between Christ and the church, and who declared that of such as little children is the Kingdom of Heaven comprised, use this book to further his purposes.

John Warwick Montgomery
December 28, 1979
The Feast of the Holy Innocents

# ACKNOWLEDGMENTS

Several (but not all) of the essays and articles contained in this book have appeared previously in theological, legal, and medical journals. The following is a bibliographical record of those earlier publications:

"How to Decide the Birth Control Question": *Christianity Today*, March 4, 1966, © 1966; *Birth Control and the Christian: a Protestant Symposium on the Control of Human Reproduction*, Walter O. Spitzer and Carlyle L. Saylor, editors (Wheaton, Ill.: Tyndale House, 1969), Appendix 5.

"Dialogue on Marriage, Divorce, and Abortion": *The Jurist* (Washington, D.C.: Catholic University of America), Winter 1975.

"American Medical Association Symposium: When Does Life Begin?": *Journal of the American Medical Association* (JAMA), Vol. 214, No. 10 (December 7, 1970), © 1970, pages 1893-95.

"The Christian View of the Fetus": *Birth Control and the Christian,* see above; *The Human Life Review,* Vol. I, No 2 (Spring 1975), abridged under the title, "The Fetus and Personhood."

"Abortion and the Law: Three Clarifications": heretofore unpublished.

"Are We in Danger of Imminent Judgment?": *Christianity Today,* January 25, 1980, © 1980, under the title, "Abortion & Imminent Judgment."

# 1: HOW TO DECIDE THE BIRTH CONTROL QUESTION

The English Renaissance exegete and saintly "Oxford reformer" John Colet, a close friend of Erasmus and Thomas More, is supposed to have remarked, "Better that no one should marry." Whereupon someone asked, "But, Dean Colet, then what would happen to the human race?" Taken aback, the Dean of St. Paul's pondered the question, then suddenly brightened and said, "Why then the end of the age and our Lord's coming could not tarry!" This tale may well be apocryphal, and certainly Colet eventually acquired a positive view of the marital state (Seebohm informs us that he advised More to marry and entrusted the control of St. Paul's school to married burghers). But the story typifies some of the confusions that have attended theological thinking on the subject of marriage and childbearing across the centuries. Christians have often manifested strange blind spots in dealing with the theology of marriage, and current discussion of birth control by both Roman Catholics and Protestants is the unwitting manifestation of a theological perplexity that extends far beyond specifics such as the "rhythm method" or "the pill."

## Roman Catholics: Marriage as a Means

The attitude of the Roman church toward birth control is well-known, though its rationale is seldom comprehended. Rome has never been happy with the principle of birth control. Limitations on childbearing in marriage are indeed permitted (preferably by sexual continence, but also today by the so-called natural rhythm method). However, such limitations are regarded as exceptions, applicable in cases of ill health, disease, acute poverty, serious temptation to sin, and so on. The use of "unnatural" (i.e., mechanical) birth-control devices stands condemned by papal decree; indeed, in 1930 the famous encyclical *Casti Connubii* declared that artificial contraception is "an unspeakable crime" and "shameful and intrinsically immoral." Widespread debate is presently going on in Roman Catholic circles over the legitimacy of the birth-control pill.[1] But the pope has as yet given no indication that the pill will be classed with "natural" birth-control methods. The pope's conservative statement of June 1964, and his reported directive to the Ecumenical Council to re-endorse the affirmations on birth control made by Popes Pius XI and XII suggest that

---

[1]For example, see Leo Pyle, editor, *The Pill and Birth Regulation: The Catholic Debate* (London: Darton, Longman and Todd, 1964).

Rome still looks with grave concern upon any techniques that would limit offspring in marriage.[2]

Critics of Rome have often gleefully pointed out the strange inconsistency that holds up the celibate state as an ideal for the clergy and at the same time seems to do all within its power to encourage childbearing on the part of the married. This is not, however, a genuine inconsistency at all, as one can see if he understands the theological base of the Roman view of marriage. Celibacy is most definitely regarded as the ideal state of life, permitting undivided attention to things spiritual (cf. the "marriage" between a nun and Christ symbolized by wedding ring and white vesture). Marriage is of value not as an end in itself, but *as a means to an end*. What end? As the *Corpus Iuris Canonici* makes clear (1013, Par. 1), and as the Holy Office reasserted in 1944 (Denzinger, 2295), the primary purpose of marriage is the generation and raising of children; other aspects of the marriage relationship must be viewed as contributory to the procreative purpose. Even the progressive Vatican II Schema 13, which endeavors to set marriage in a more Christocentric framework, twice states that "matrimony and conjugal love are by their very nature ordained for the procreation and education of children." Rome is thus quite consistent in making every effort to discourage birth control, and in taking particularly strong measures against all attempts to limit birth by techniques in opposition to the "natural law" doctrine fundamental to all Thomistic theology.

The traditional Roman view of marriage and birth control has been a source of embarrassment to its advocates and a fruitful base for criticism by moderns who resent religious authority. It is pointed out that, pragmatically, fewer and fewer Roman Catholics

[2]See *Christianity Today*, December 17, 1965, p. 34.

accept the procreative "marriage as means" interpretation of their Church. Thus in a 1956 survey of the marital relationships of English women, Chesser found that of his sample of Roman Catholics, 47 percent were practicing birth control. And in 1959 Freedman and his associates, in investigating the contraceptive practices of American wives, discovered that even among the Roman Catholics who were regular churchgoers, 26 percent were using birth-control devices considered gravely sinful by the Church.

The application of "natural law" thinking to the birth-control issue seems especially bizarre, since it is difficult to see why man can legitimately control "natural" phenomena such as vegetation and animal population, and yet cannot without sin control his own numbers in the face of severe population pressures. As one writer has put it, a fixed law of nature dictates that male Caucasians grow hair on their faces; but it is not sinful to use a razor— whether straight or electric! And why is the use of mechanical contraceptives more "unnatural" than the application of the rhythm method? The latter obviously creates an unnatural pressure on the married couple to restrain their desire during one phase of the menstrual cycle, whereas the use of contraceptives or birth-control pills permits intercourse when natural desire dictates. The rhythm method, according to Dr. John Rock of the Harvard Medical School, himself a Roman Catholic, "is to be considered an unnatural method, for it is during the fertile period that the whole psychosomatic psychology of the healthy, normal female is prepared and intended by her primate nature for coitus."[3]

[3]John Rock, *Medical and Biological Aspects of Contraception* (Boston: Lippincott, 1943).

## Secularists and Liberal Protestants: Marriage as an End

More important, however, than these specific objections to the Roman Catholic theology of birth control has been the rise of a very different philosophy of marriage in modern times. This is the view, nourished by the courtly love tradition of the medieval period and the romantic movement of the nineteenth century, that sees the union of man and woman not as a means to an end, but as an end in itself. The twentieth-century ideological shift from essentialist to existentialist patterns of thought has greatly accentuated the new view of man-woman relationships. As the distinguished French medical scholar Chauchard puts it, "To speak of natural law is to produce an easy indifference. Modern man sees himself as free. . . . He refuses every constraint."[4] When combined with a thinly disguised contemporary humanism, the result is a sex ethic (not limited to marriage) that sees in the love relation per se the fulfillment of human aspirations and the manifestation of God-as-Agape. Thus we arrive at the so-called new morality of J. A. T. Robinson and the permissive sex ethics of numerous moderns—philosophies that, in radical contrast with Roman Catholicism, absolutize the love relation with hardly a second look at procreation.

The attitude toward birth control arising from such an existentialist-humanistic context is easily predictable: birth control is no longer a theological problem. "We are faced with a problem that must be solved at the purely biological level."[5] The ethics of birth control becomes situational and *ad hoc*. As a car sticker my wife

---

[4]Paul Chauchard, *Apprendre à aimer: régulation des naissances et morale sexuelle* (Paris: Fayard, 1963), p. 62.

[5]David J. McCallion, "Human Population Pressures and Birth Control," *Canadian Journal of Theology*, July 1960.

saw expressed it: "Trouble Parking? Try Planned Parenthood."
The overpopulation issue engulfs birth-control thinking, result-
in weird volumes such as retired Army Colonel Alexander J.
Stuart's *Overpopulation—Twentieth Century Nemesis: A Con-
densed, Objective Study of Procreation—from the Amoeba to
Modern Man.*[6] Even a respectable work like *The Population Ex-
plosion and Christian Responsibility*[7] by Richard Fagley, an offi-
cial spokesman for the World Council of Churches, focuses chief
attention on the economic and technological aspects of population
growth and sees the ecumenical movement, with its united wit-
ness to an overpopulated world, as "the way forward."

Though liberal Protestants and secularists have readily identi-
fied the erroneous reasoning in Roman Catholic birth-control doctrine, they have, strange to say, fallen into a more acute form of
the same error. Roman Catholic "natural law" thinking is a variety of what G. E. Moore in his *Principia Ethica* called the "naturalistic fallcy": the assumption that the descriptive (what is) automatically gives rise to the normative (what ought to be). But the
liberals commit this same blunder with far less "justification"
(since they have neither absolute church nor inerrant Scripture to
interpret nature for them). The overpopulation problem in itself
does not establish the morality of birth control, any more than it
would establish the morality of war as a means of reducing the
population. And the situational ethic of *agape*-love, as I have
emphasized in my essay "The Law's Third Use:
Sanctification,"[8] and in my debate with Joseph Fletcher,[9] leaves

[6](New York: Exposition, 1958).

[7](New York: Oxford, 1960).

[8]John Warwick Montgomery, *Crisis in Lutheran Theology.* I (Minneapolis:
Bethany, 1973), 124-27.

[9]Joseph Fletcher and John Warwick Montgomery, *Situation Ethics: True or
False?* (Minneapolis: Bethany, 1972).

man with no guideline for the content of ethical action. Love is a motive, not a structure, and one makes a severe logical "category mistake" to think that it can serve both functions. A reliable revelation of God's divine will is *sine qua non* for man's ethical decisions in the realm of marriage and birth control, as in all other areas of life. In Holy Scripture, one has the key to interpret God's hand in nature and human life and the guideline for love's operations.

## Biblical Christianity: Marriage as Analogy

And how does the Bible view the problem area we are confronting? To answer this question, we must move beyond proof-texting to the focal center of scriptural teaching on marriage. This center is not to be found in the first two chapters of Genesis, so often cited in isolation, but in Ephesians 5:22-33, which quotes Genesis in the context of the New Covenant in Christ. Understood in the light of New Testament fulfillment, marriage cannot be regarded simply as a means ("Be fruitful, and multiply, and replenish the earth") or unqualifiedly as an end ("They shall be one flesh"). Rather, it is seen as an *analogy*—indeed, as the best human analogy—of the relationship between Christ and his church. After having connected husband-and-wife with Christ-and-the-church by no less than three *hōs's* ("as") and two *kathōs's* ("just as") in eleven verses, Paul concludes with a summary statement on the marriage relation: "This is a great mystery: but I speak concerning Christ and the church." When, and only when, marriage is viewed as the type of which Christ-and-church are antitype can we avoid the Hegelian-like dialectic extremes of the Roman and liberal Protestant views of marriage and birth control. Specifically:

23

1. As Christ's relation with the church is a *total* love relation, not just a means to an end, so one must not view marriage simply as a procreative function. Where birth control can contribute to "subduing the earth" in order to achieve a better total human relationship, it is not to be condemned.[10] By the same token, the psychosomatic wholeness implied in Christ's incarnation for man's salvation condemns the Manichaean and Neoplatonic depreciation of the flesh that colors so much of Roman Catholic celibacy teaching. No better counteractive exists to all such functional misunderstandings of marriage than the writings of Charles Williams, the late Christian poet and friend of C. S. Lewis (Shideler well titles her treatment of Williams's thought *The Theology of Romantic Love*).

2. Yet neither is the human love relationship an end in itself. "In the resurrection they neither marry, nor are given in marriage."[11] Why? Because "when that which is perfect is come, then that which is in part shall be done away."[12] In the full manifestation of the antitype, the type is embraced and disappears. Thus the love-relationship between male and female must never be absolutized. It is truly meaningful only insofar as it reflects the Christ-relationship. Apart from this it becomes idolatrous, taking on demonic quality despite its lack of genuine ultimacy. The present state of American mores and morals is sufficient evidence of the appalling consequences that attend the isolation of sex from God's revealed will.

3. In light of the divine analogy of marriage, we can see the centrality of children to marital union. Christ did not give himself

---

[10]Cf. William E. Hulme, "A Theological Approach to Birth Control." *Pastoral Psychology*, April 1960.

[11]Matthew 22:30.

[12]1 Corinthians 13:10.

up to death as an isolated deed; he did it to "bring many sons unto glory."[13] As the union of Christ and his church does not exist for its own sake, but to bring others to spiritual rebirth, so the marital union is properly fulfilled in natural birth. And since natural birth precedes spiritual birth, as creation precedes redemption,[14] so the Christian home can be the greatest single agency for nurture in the twofold sense; thus did the Reformers view it.[15] The burden of proof rests, then, on the couple who wish to restrict the size of their family; to the extent possible and desirable, all Christian couples should seek to "bring many sons unto glory." After all, as C. G. Darwin pointed out at the University of Chicago's Darwin centennial, those who restrict their birthrate will ultimately be engulfed by those who do not: *"Homo contracipiens* would become extinct and would be replaced by the variety *Homo progenetivus."* The Christian application of this principle is obvious.

4. Sexual relations outside marriage are unqualifiedly to be condemned, not for the naturalistic (and logically questionable!) reasons set forth by Bertocci,[16] but because they violate the high analogy of Christ-and-church. Thus Israel's prostitution of God's grace through idolatry was symbolized by Hosea's wife, who lived as a woman of the street, and Paul expresses revulsion at the thought of those who are "members of Christ" becoming "one flesh" with harlots, thereby violating the temple of the Holy Spirit.[17] The crux of Paul's argument against illicit sex is the

---

[13]Hebrews 2:10.

[14]John 3:3-12.

[15]Cf. William H. Lazareth, *Luther on the Christian Home* (Philadelphia: Muhlenberg, 1960).

[16]Peter Bertocci, "Extramarital Sex and the Pill," *The Christian Century,* February 26, 1964.

[17]1 Corinthians 6:13-20.

analogy relation—that Christians "are bought with a price." So the use of birth-control devices outside of marriage is not to be tolerated. And the hypocrisy of gas-station dispensers "for prevention of disease" is to be made clear in no uncertain terms.

How practically are Christian marriage partners to decide the birth-control question? Within the framework of the analogy relation, they are to consider it personally and prayerfully in light of their own physical, emotional, financial, and spiritual situation, and in light of the population picture in their area of the world. (The answer will not be the same for Christians in India and those in Canada; for those led to lucrative vocations and those led to pioneer missionary work.) They will act responsibly, remembering that irresponsibility is equally possible at the Roman Catholic antibirth-control and the secularistic probirth-control extremes. Viewing marriage as neither means nor end, but as the great analogy of Christ's work of salvation, the Christian will seek to do all he can to make his marriage evangelistic—generatively and regeneratively. He will consider with all seriousness such proposals as that made by the Rev. Eldon Durham, who, in the face of the severe and rapidly growing population problem in so many parts of the world, advocates that Christians "begin to constitute families by means of adopting the unwanted, the disinherited, the dispossessed and the rejected children" of the earth.[18] Though such a suggestion must not be used to justify nonchildbearing in American marriages and irresponsibility or immorality on the part of couples living elsewhere in the world, is not the proposal genuinely analogous to the "grafting" of the Gentiles unto the tree of salvation?[19] Surely the childless Christian couple is here

[18]*Time*, December 3, 1965, p. 77.
[19]Romans 11.

offered a superlative privilege and opportunity.

But however he is led to fulfill his personal responsibility before the Lord of the church, the Christian stands free from the shackles of legalism and from the chaos of libertarianism. "If the Son shall make you free," said Jesus, "ye shall be free indeed."[20] On the basis of this merciful freedom in Christ, the apostle beseeches us as a reasonable act of worship to present our bodies "a living sacrifice holy, acceptable unto God."[21]

[20]John 8:36.
[21]Romans 12:1

# 2: DIALOGUE ON MARRIAGE, DIVORCE, AND ABORTION*

It used to be said that the only thing all Protestants had in common was their dislike of Roman Catholics. That isn't the case anymore, of course, and as background for my remarks, it probably would help for you to know, generally, what my theology is. A few remarks may also prevent those here in theology from expending energy trying to induce what my position is from what

*The following presentation was given by invitation at a symposium on "Recent Developments in American Family Law and Their Implications for Traditional Religious Values." This was sponsored by The Catholic University of America's Center for Law and Religious Traditions and held at The Catholic University of America School of Law on April 12, 1975. The afternoon session of the symposium featured a panel discussion and open forum, an edited transcription of which

I say subsequently. I am what C. S. Lewis called an "old Western man." That is, I hold to a definite and articulate revelation of God which has established certain principles beyond dispute. I operate revelationally in dealing with questions of the kind which have come up in this conference.

I was delighted with the paper of Professor Zuckman largely because toward the end of his paper he moves beyond the narrow issues of no-fault divorce codes to the general issue of what is happening to marriage in our culture. He quite rightly finds the locus of divorce at the weakening of the marriage relationship

---

follows Dr. Montgomery's presentation. The principal contributors to this panel discussion were:

PROFESSOR HARVEY L. ZUCKMAN. a member of the faculty of The Catholic University of America School of Law. His areas of specialization include domestic relations, conflicts of laws, torts, and communications. He is Vice-chairman. Family and Juvenile Law Section, Association of American Law Schools.

MSGR. JAMES T. MCHUGH. Director of the Secretariat of the Pro-life Activities Committee of the National Conference of Catholic Bishops. and former Director of the Family Life Division of the Committee on Education of the United States Catholic Conference.

PROFESSOR JOSEPH P. WITHERSPOON. the Thomas Shelton Maxey Professor of Law at the University of Texas School of Law. His areas of specialization are jurisprudence, civil rights, administrative law, and constitutional law. He is an associate editor of *The American Journal of Jurisprudence*.

DR. JULIA REGAN MARCIN. graduate of Georgetown University Medical School. She completed her internship and residency in Hartford. Connecticut. and is employed at present by the Howard County (Maryland) Public Health Department.

REV. CHARLES E. CURRAN. Professor of Theology in the School of Religious Studies of The Catholic University of America. He has published numerous books and articles on Christian ethics.

PROFESSOR JOHN WARWICK MONTGOMERY. then professor of law and theology at the International School of Law in Washington. D.C.

PROFESSOR VIRGINIA EASLEY DEMARCE. a member of the faculty of George Mason University in Fairfax, Virginia. who served as moderator. Her interests include church. legal. administrative. social. and family history. She is a Bible-believer and Wisconsin Synod Lutheran.

30

and not at the type of divorce legislation which happens to exist. It is much too simplistic to think that the no-fault divorce laws bring about a weakening of the marriage relationship. Professor Zuckman quite properly emphasizes that the problem is much deeper. I think his use of Epstein was particularly appropriate. Epstein is absolutely correct that the movement toward self-centrism in our culture is the causative factor responsible for most fundamental problems in marriage today. The proper context for evaluating no-fault divorce is to see it as a sub-issue in our response to contemporary self-centrism.

I enjoyed and concur with Msgr. McHugh's prefatory remarks. His belief that no-fault divorce has definite advantages in certain situations in no way detracts from his conviction that we need to hold to the absolutes as far as the permanence of marriage is concerned. It seems to me that any dealing with no-fault divorce within a Christian context must be understood that way. First we have to determine what the absolutes are relative to the marital union. Then we have to see pragmatically what our cultural situation is. Finally we have to ask ourselves: how can we best effectuate these moral absolutes within the particular situation in which we find ourselves? Phrased from a different perspective, we have to avoid two gross errors. One of them is a kind of mechanical absolutism which insists upon enforcing revelational standards on a society which is largely pluralistic at the present time, and doesn't, by its own personal conviction, reflect these standards. And the other error is that of the situationist who finds it hard to focus on any absolute standard at all, and feels that somehow ethical issues are going to resolve themselves through the situation itself.[1]

---

[1]Cf. Joseph Fletcher and John Warwick Montgomery, *Situation Ethics: True or False?* (Minneapolis: Bethany, 1972).

Now, in light of my feelings toward both of those papers, what do I think of the divorce issue? I think no-fault divorce is a good direction for the law to take as long as there is mandatory counseling in most instances and a mandatory waiting period. How is it that I take that view if I am convinced, as I am, that marriage is properly indissoluble and that Scripture gives only one ground for divorce, namely, adultery? Here we have to make a distinction among sins. There are sins of such a nature that they cut to the very heart of society; and if these become a matter of common acceptance, they make it impossible for society to function. There are other kinds of sins which do not have that kind of result, though they may very well carry severe eternal consequences for the person involved. I am convinced that the taking of the defenseless human life, as occurs in abortion, is a sin of the former variety and thus that abortion should be opposed with all the ammunition we have to bring to it. I think Professor Witherspoon is so terribly right in his judgment on this situation; namely, that it is the gravest moral issue of our day, perhaps the gravest constitutional issue our country has ever faced. But I don't think that divorce in our society is a problem of equivalent magnitude.

Why? Not because the family isn't of crucial importance. The family—the very idea of family—is what the Reformers called an "order of creation" (*Schöpfungsordnung*). We don't have society without some sort of familial organization. It is what Emil Brunner refers to in *The Divine Imperative* as one of the essential, defining elements of a society.[2] But there isn't just one possible type of marriage. We are moving from a traditional monogamy to what one wag has called "serial monogamy," that is, not being

---

[2]Cf. John Warwick Montgomery, *Jurisprudence: A Book of Readings*, 2nd edition (Strasbourg, France: International Scholarly Publishers, 1980), Pt. 3, B.

married to more than one person at any one time. This is the Hollywood approach to marriage: today you are married to only one person, but next week it may be someone else; your marital partner certainly need not be the same person throughout your entire life. I am convinced that this is antirevelational. God does not like that sort of thing if Scripture says anything. On the other hand, serial monogamy is a fact of our culture. A society could be structured that way and presumably survive. Our Lord says, in reference to divorce, that certain actions were permitted "because of the hardness of your hearts" even though it was not the ideal: "from the beginning it was not so."[3] Society can operate on less than the best of God's standards. If that is the case, and we find ourselves in a pluralistic society which is moving away from God's standards, then the questions come to the Christian: How hard should we try to force the non-Christian to accord with God's highest standards on a matter like divorce? What are the consequences if we insist on it?

Let me give you an analogy. There is a Christian college in the South (it shall remain nameless) which was responsible for the creation of the small town around. The college owns the land on which the town is located and also the water rights of the town. Some years ago a gentleman moved into this town and started a laundry business. He chose to have his shop open on Sunday. The town council consisted of members of the college and they informed him that he certainly could stay open on Sunday, but that his water would be cut off. Now the town had every right to do this—every legal right that is. The question in situations like this is not whether Sunday closing is scriptural—a moot point which I won't argue—but rather how Christians should interact with our

[3]Matthew 19:3-9.

pluralistic society. Even assuming that Sunday closing is scriptur-
ally required, what effect does it have on the non-Christian
(assuming that the businessman was a non-Christian) to force him
to conform to Scripture? Isn't it possible in such a situation to win
the argument and lose the soul? He goes to Hell forced to have
aligned his actions with Sunday closing laws! Maybe under those
circumstances it would be better for us to take a little lighter
approach and not grind down so hard.

I am suggesting that in a society where most people are now
getting married on a non-Christian basis, we make a great mistake
if we insist on their being divorced only on a scriptural basis. The
no-fault divorce, I think, becomes a lesser of evils in a society
such as ours. Of course, we ought to push as hard as we can to
alter the climate of opinion in the direction of a proper view—
"proper" equaling "revelational." But ultimately that will come
about only if society changes its fundamental convictions. Such a
fundamental change requires no less than *conversion*. To bring
about that kind of alteration in the climate of opinion, we would
have to demonstrate in some independent fashion (such as demonstrating the credentials of revelation) that adultery ought to be the
only acceptable reason for divorce.

In light of this, it seems to me that the best solution to the
no-fault issue is to have two parallel ways of obtaining a divorce,
one of them the traditional fault system, the other a no-fault
system. Here I part company with Professor Zuckman, but I don't
think he will be too disturbed by it. It seems to me that it would
certainly be possible to have the old fault system operate without
in any way muddying the waters of the no-fault system. He com-
plains, quite rightly, that unfortunately "the single biggest problem presented by the 'add on' approach is that it leaves intact the
entire fault system with respect to the collateral issues arising out

of a nonfault divorce,'' that is, division of the property and custody of the children. I don't see that it would have to. It should be possible to have two systems operating in a parallel fashion. A person could either go on a fault basis or a no-fault basis without one necessarily disturbing the other. This would make it possible for those who have entered marriage on a nonrevelational basis to sever the bonds on the same basis. At the same time, it would be possible for those people who are trying to operate on a revelational basis to obtain a divorce on a legitimate revelational ground.

Now one might still say: couldn't we dispense with the fault system in the civil law and expect that to be handled by the churches? Wouldn't it be possible to have parallel civil and ecclesiastical divorce on the model of the European civil and ecclesiastical marriage? The answer to this is that it certainly would be possible, but insofar as we are able to retain a recognition of revelational standards in our legal system, we ought to do so. There is no point in giving away any more ground than we absolutely have to as long as we still leave a path open to those people who need to operate on a different standard. The tendency in our current legal system—in our current jurisprudence, if you will—is to separate or remove entirely the notions of guilt, sin, and blame from the legal sphere. Perhaps the high watermark of *mens rea,* the guilty mind, has passed. The law now tries to operate with minimum attention to the category of guilt. I believe that we ought to try to retain that theme in the law insofar as we can. Interestingly enough, it has been shown that Augustine was the source of the *mens rea* concept as it entered into the European civil law and from there into our common law.[4] The direction

---

[4]Sir Alfred Denning, *The Changing Law* (London: Stevens, 1953), p. 112.

given by our revelational source in the area of divorce is quite obvious and clear.[5] Thus we ought to retain as much of it as possible in the law. At the same time, we ought to give the opportunity to a person who is not living in terms of Christian revelation to break a marriage commitment which certainly is hurting him more than it is helping.

Now a word or two on the abortion issue. It doesn't seem to me that this issue should focus on the putative father's rights. Not that I think Professor Witherspoon or my other fellow-panelists are suggesting that at all, but the way in which the agenda for the conference has been set up might give the impression that the father's rights are the focal center of the problem. They certainly aren't. The most recent legislation and court decisions have made it plain that the father is not going to play a decisive role in this issue. The issue must be met squarely on the question as to whether, when we deal with the fetus, we are dealing with a human being. That is the issue Blackmun and the Court tried to sidestep in *Roe v. Wade* and yet decided in the negative by implication. The question is squarely whether the fetus at the moment of conception actually is a person subject to the same rights and privileges as any person subsequent to birth.

The people who have written on this issue in recent years from the standpoint of "right to life" are absolutely correct when they assert that human life is totally present at that point. At France's National Center for Scientific Research, Jules Carles, one of the foremost geneticists of our time, has pointed out that the whole genetic package—the entire chromosomal pattern—is established at the moment of conception. From there on nothing but nida-

---

[5]See note 3 above.

tion—nesting and nutriment—takes place.[6] Only food has to come in from that point on. There is no point where, plunk, something is later inserted which turns out to be the human being. Indeed, our medieval forefathers were just identifying the first evidence of life that they could conclusively detect when they talked about quickening as the beginning of life. They were saying that as soon as you had life, there must be protection for it.[7] Now we know that life starts at the moment of conception with nothing superadded.

The only thing left is the value question: what are we going to do with human life once we have it? Heaven help us—literally—if we answer that question in the negative, because then we can place a negative valuation on human life in other "helpless" forms too, can't we? We can with equal justification place a negative value on the aged, on the mentally retarded, or perhaps even on those we don't care for racially. Thus the value question becomes a matter of the most extreme consequences.

I'm afraid I can't go along with Dr. Marcin's view that nondirective therapy is the physician's proper role in the abortion decision. A matter of highest principle is involved and therefore the physician's counseling role here, if the physician has his head screwed on right, ought to be directed toward preserving the life of that human being who cannot defend himself.[8] I agree with Dr.

---

[6] Jules Carles, *La fécondation*, 5th edition (Paris: Presses Universitaires de France, 1967), pp. 81-82.

[7] Cf. Robert M. Byrn, "Goodbye to the Judeo-Christian Era in Law," *America*, June 2, 1973, p. 512.

[8] "Julia and Raymond Marcin are generally opposed to liberalized abortion and specifically opposed to the majority opinion in *Roe* and *Doe*. The focus of their paper was not what a physician's role should be when confronted with a request for an abortion (the question to which Dr. Montgomery addresses himself) but rather, drawing from *Roe* and *Doe* and subsequent cases on the same subject, what the court visualizes as the physician's role." (Editors of *The Jurist*)

37

Marcin that it is terribly unfortunate that so many pregnant girls are receiving directive counseling by "the narrow partisanship of committed young women who have had abortions." In Dr. Nathanson's view (whom Dr. Marcin quotes), the kind of counseling that pregnant women contemplating abortion are presently receiving is "decidedly directive." I think that is very unfortunate, but I don't think the answer is to move from directive to nondirective counseling, à la Carl Rogers. This would be to throw out the baby—or fetus—with the bath water. The result of trying to help the counselee get "in touch with her own feelings" may accomplish no more than to put her in touch with some very dubious feelings or a misdirected value system. Insofar as it is possible to help a woman see what is really happening—that she is responsible for a genuine human life—I think directive counseling is mandatory. Certainly that is the responsibility of any Christian physician.

*Panel Discussion*

ZUCKMAN:

Let me exercise my privilege as a member of the panel to start off. I find so little disagreement on the question of no-fault divorce on this panel that I'm not going to spend much time on it other than to respond to Professor Montgomery in this regard. I think it should be possible for people who follow the revelational view to have their divorce process at the same time as the no-fault civil process. I could visualize a situation with a fault and a no-fault system operating side by side. Perhaps the parties broke up because of their differences over religion, and one could go in the no-fault door and the other the fault door of the court. Both could get a divorce. Now I'm not saying that would be so terrible. We've had that kind of situation in California before no-fault divorce. Recrimination as a defense was struck down, and both parties could get a divorce. But I would suggest that there might be some difficulties with that approach.


McHUGH:

I want to respond to Dr. Montgomery: you suggest this twofold system of divorce—fault on the one hand and no-fault on the other. You suggest that as a possible system, and I don't think Professor Zuckman took you up on that issue significantly. I would like to. I don't think your system is possible. I think the crux of the debate over fault v. no-fault divorce is whether they can exist together. There are difficulties with the present system; there are weaknesses in it. But what we are asking for is not a change in the code, but a change in philosophy. You can't change the philosophy and let the two systems survive together. That's the crux of the debate between the ABA (American Bar Association) and the framers of the Uniform Marriage and Divorce Act. In a former paper I said, and I would just like to read this: "The basic definition of 'irretrievable breakdown' must be achieved if no-fault divorce is to be a just and humane replacement for traditional divorce laws."[9] Once traditional grounds of fault concepts are introduced, even simply as corroboration of the breakdown, the judges, lawyers, and the parties begin to think in the old categories. They are no longer thinking of the breakdown of the marriage, whether it is in fact irretrievably broken, whether in fact

[9]James T. McHugh, editor, *Marriage in the Light of Vatican II* (Washington, D.C.: Family Life Bureau, U.S.C.C., 1968).

39

it is better for the two people, for the children, and for society for the couple to separate. They are rather thinking how do we manipulate this situation so as to get them apart from one another regardless of our responsibilities to the couple, to the children, and to society. I submit that to reintroduce fault is a cop-out. Furthermore, the commentary on the UMDA makes it clear that new terms and procedures are called for in order to disassociate divorce from the fault orientation. In the words of the commentary, the precise reason for the change in form and words is "to impress the bench and bar with the break from past concepts."[10] I think that is exactly the problem that we're facing today in the legislatures. They are copping out by either adding "irretrievable breakdown" to the existing grounds, or they are trying to bottle the two systems as one.

For my money divorce is bad. It is bad for everyone involved. It is bad for society. But if it is going to exist, and unfortunately it seems that it is, then we ought to have a system that respects human dignity and safeguards the dignity of marriage and the rights of children. I don't think you have that under the existing system. I think there is the *capacity* to have it under a good no-fault system. I think that the tinkering with the no-fault concept going on in the legislatures and courts today is unworthy of anyone who has a concern for the law.


DeMarce:

Everybody here has been assuming that marriage is more or less an identical case for all. I am wondering if, in the light of the relationship between law and religious traditions which we've

[10]Uniform Marriage and Divorce Law, Part III. ¶301, Comment.

seen here, it would be possible to have a divorce system in which the court has an obligation to look at what the married couple really promised in the first place when getting married. I have attended weddings, I must say, in which I have heard them take vows by which they do swear to live together so long as they shall love one another. In this context, it seems to me, if the law is willing to concede the dysfunctioning of the marriage—the loss of love—it ought to be reasonably easy to obtain a divorce on the grounds of irretrievable breakdown. On the other hand, if the law really wants to take seriously the fact that they stood there and swore that they would stay married until the death of one of them, the law should make divorce considerably more difficult. I don't think the law should be able to make the nature of the agreement clear only when a party wants to dissolve the relationship if the law has allowed the nature of the agreement to be obscured when it was entered into.

ZUCKMAN:

Well, I'll just respond very quickly to that point. I think that at some point Professor Montgomery ought to respond to Msgr. McHugh on this dual system. I might agree with you if the law allowed individuals to fashion their own marriage contract. It does not. That is the thrust of Dr. Jessie Bernard's work, *The Future of Marriage,*[11] in which she said that is what eventually will happen. We are no longer going to have the permanent, lifelong marriage contract. The parties will have a choice. Then I think we should hold the parties to their contracts. I happen to be a firm believer in living up to one's contracts. But where a couple is

[11] Jessie Bernard, *The Future of Marriage* (New York: Bantam Books, 1973).

41

forced into one type of contract almost as if dealing with a car salesman and is confronted with boilerplate take-it-or-leave-it language, I don't think the law should hold people to that contract.

MONTGOMERY:

Yes, there are different languages being spoken by the parties involved. There is a certain amount of "sales puffing" that takes place in domestic law.

DeMARCE:

One thing I'd like to emphasize is the need for education of people of high school age and younger about the reality of marriage and the consequences of the sexual act. A lot of the problems we are discussing today might be resolved by placing the emphasis on educating people beforehand rather than trying to pick up the pieces after the fact.

CURRAN:

Dr. Montgomery, I'd like to disagree with your view on the advisability of a dual divorce system. It seems to me that the reason I disagree is that in the last analysis your view and my view of the legal order are different. You frame the legal order in terms of there being only one way people should act and if people are not able to live up to this standard, then you would tolerate the lesser evil, either forcing people to outwardly observe the standard or allowing them to fall short of it. Now frankly this is what I dubbed the "old approach" within the Roman Catholic theology. The "old approach" is an attempt to make the legal law mirror the moral law. My own position holds for much more separation between the moral and legal order and for an acceptance of the fact of a pluralistic society. The function of civil law is to give as much freedom to the individual as possible and only to intervene when necessary in terms of the demand for public order.

McHUGH:

I would think there must be more to the function of law than that. Father Curran, you talk about the protection of public order and you set out three criteria—peace, justice, and morality. You cannot separate people's values, which are based in their religious convictions or their philosophic convictions or their world-view, from what they think is right and wrong. In a democratic society where people have the right to express themselves on the formulation of law, you cannot divorce the values generally held in society from those espoused by the law, even if society's values are generally based in religious convictions or religious world-views. My problem with Father Curran's approach is that he seems to be saying, "freedom for the individual to the maximum degree possible." That begins to reduce the law to a simply regulatory function, depriving it of the possibility to enunciate values. In most of our social legislation now we are enunciating values, values about the dignity and worth of the human person. The corresponding obligation of society is to supply help and support to the underprivileged, the old, and those in special need. I think it is an important function of the law to enunciate values, and that includes the law of marital and familial relationships.

MRS. VIRGINIA HEFFERNAN:

Two years ago I was sent down to the Maryland legislature to listen to their interpretation of the area of concern, of Maryland marriage and divorce laws. According to those speaking, the civil law was only concerned about the protection of property rights and children. Otherwise, it seemed, marriage was of no consequence to the law. I would like a legal opinion as to the reality of the situation.

MCHUGH:

Let me put in this footnote, Mrs. Heffernan. I don't think you can get an exclusively legal opinion about the function of civil laws. To do so would automatically give civil law primacy over moral law.

HEFFERNAN:

My concern for the legal opinion about the function of civil marriage and divorce laws stems from listening to much testimony in the Maryland legislature given by divorced people. The strikingly recurring theme of their testimony was that a legal divorce boils down to a big hassle over property and custody rights of the children. I would like a lawyer's reflection on this situation.

ZUCKMAN:

Well, I guess I'm elected. The whole idea of contract in marriage came out of the Roman law and was modified by English ecclesiastical law. The contractual relationship of the parties gave rise to a status. Contrary to the teaching of the Catholic Church on the indissolubility of marriage, our courts decided very early to allow divorce. If you are going to allow divorce, the change of status is accomplished simply by judicial decree. The parties have already dissolved their own interpersonal relationship, and what you are left with then is the children's custody and property settlement. The emphasis in the court on property and child custody is the practical approach to dealing with the only contested remnants of the defunct marriage.

The procedures for handling a divorce have historical roots. The legislatures are trying to grapple with this historicity in terms of the here and now. We can be critical of the legislature as much as we want, and I'm as critical as any, but we still have to realize that they are grappling every session with all sorts of other social problems and they are going to take the here and now before the long view.

DeMARCE:

From the perspective of a historian, I think it is also important to realize that the Maryland legislature was looking at those aspects of marriage which were traditionally within the province of the secular courts in the Middle Ages. There is no doubt whatsoever that the traditional marriage contract was regarded primarily as an economic relationship not so much between the two spouses as between the two families. The necessary precondition for a marriage in any property-holding family was the contract which specified dower and curtsy and which specified precisely what each family was going to contribute to the venture. Naturally, when the contract dissolved, this was the only aspect of it that the secular courts tended to be interested in. The rest was the province of the ecclesiastical courts.

45

ERNEST PIERUCCI:

Professor Zuckman, the Supreme Court's opinion in *Loving v. Virginia*[12] seems to be permeated with the view that marriage is the arch upon which society builds. The law has always recognized, at least to the extent of my reading in law school, that marriage, the family, is the central element of society. I would trust that when legislatures sit down to write marriage and divorce laws they consider not only property matters, but also the importance of marriage to the structure of society. Was this your experience in Missouri and Maryland?

ZUCKMAN:

I found it to be the case more in Missouri than in Maryland. I don't know why there was the difference. (I think my role in Missouri was grossly overstated earlier.) I presented a statement on divorce reform in Missouri in favor of a UMDA-type statute even before it had been actually finalized. Missouri passed something more like the English reform where divorce is granted if there is a "breakdown" of the marriage, but "breakdown" is defined in terms of adultery, desertion, cruelty, and the other standard faults. But I would hope so, too: I would hope that they had broad societal values in mind when framing the law. I think that *Loving v. Virginia,* a Supreme Court case, is a very good and eloquent statement in defense of the family. But I think legislatures are inclined to take that sort of information as background and then try to confront the specific, primarily economic, problems that arise out of the marriage contract and its dissolution. I

[12]*Loving v. Virginia,* 388 U.S. 1, 87 S. Ct. 1817, 18 L. Ed. 2d 1010 (1967).

imagine the legislators hope that the practical solutions they present will square with the general philosophy that the family is the cornerstone of our society.

Going back to the papers presented this morning, however, my primary concern, I think, is with Professor Witherspoon's presentation. Now I will state at the outset that I disagree with a great deal of what Professor Witherspoon says. I do want to indicate my agreement on one point. I think that you do not persuade your adversary by silencing him. I agree wholeheartedly with the idea that the views expressed by Professor Witherspoon should have their day in court. I don't think that a democracy and a free judicial system should deny anyone their view, or the opportunity to express their view.

But I would say this. I take exception to the characterization of the majority of the Court in *Roe* and *Doe* as having prostituted the constitutional process. I don't believe that for a moment. I've had the privilege of arguing before Justice Blackmun many times while he was a Court of Appeals judge. I could find no more conscientious judge, no judge more concerned about the constitutional process in this country. And so though I don't think the Supreme Court needs any defense, I would indicate that I would disassociate myself from Professor Witherspoon's view. Maybe the Court was wrong. I think Professor Witherspoon ought to have the opportunity to persuade them of that. I happen to think the Court was right. I hope that as a member of the faculty of the host university I don't sound discourteous, Professor Witherspoon.

In addition, I'd just like to point out that Professor Witherspoon nominated *Roe* and *Doe* for the worst constitutional cases that he's ever come across. My nomination is one that was not discussed today, but could well have been included in this conference, a case called *Labine v. Vincent*[13] in which the Supreme Court made me very angry. It disenfranchised, if you will, illegitimate children from inheriting from their parents because they were illegitimate, even though they had been acknowledged prior to the death of their parents. I think you can see from my disagreement with that case and my agreement with the Supreme Court generally in *Roe* and *Doe* that my concern begins at the point of birth.

WITHERSPOON:

Madam Chairman, may I correct the record if it isn't correct already. I intended to use the term "prostitution" with respect to the decision in *Dred Scott*. I am not the first to have used it. I've used it with respect to Judge Pettine's decision concerning the standing of unborn children and the fathers of unborn children, and keeping both the unborn children and their guardians and fathers, members of plaintiff's class in *Roe* and *Doe*, out of court.[14] If I used the term "prostitution" of the constitutional adjudication process in reference to the Court in *Roe* and *Doe* I don't recall it, but that makes little difference, I'll use it now. I think it was a prostitution of the constitutional adjudication process. I say it for one reason, and that reason Professor Zuckman knows. He is familiar with *Everson v. Board of Education*.[15] I pick that case for stating what it is that the Supreme Court is

---

[13]*Labine v. Vincent*, 401 U.S. 532, 91 S. Ct. 1017, 28 L. Ed. 2d 288 (1971); rehearing denied 402 U.S. 990, 91 S. Ct. 72, 29 L. Ed. 2d 156 (1971).

[14]*Doe v. Israel*, 358 F. Supp. 1193 (R.I. 1973).

[15]*Everson v. Board of Education*, 330 U.S. 1, 67 S. Ct. 504, 91 L. Ed. 711 (1947).

supposed to do when it assigns a meaning to a constitutional provision. It is the same case in which Mr. Justice Black, who was no mean justice in my opinion (perhaps after the first Mr. Justice Harlan and Chief Justice Marshall, the greatest judge who sat on that Court in terms of civil and political rights, a judge who had to educate himself on the Court and took his job seriously), said the fundamental obligation of the Supreme Court in administering a constitutional provision is to determine the meaning and scope of the language in which it is expressed, and I quote from *Everson,* "in light of its history and the evils it was designed to suppress, the purpose its framers had in view and the understanding of the meaning of that language by those who fashioned and adopted it." We find that in *Everson v. Board of Education,* 330 U.S. 1, 8, 15-16 (1947). I say to you, Mr. Zuckman, that the Supreme Court in *Roe v. Wade* made no move, assigned no effort, to discovering the actual purpose of the framers of the Fourteenth and Thirteenth Amendments with respect to the beings they sought to protect by the safeguards of due process, equal protection of the laws, and the prohibition of slavery and involuntary servitude. Not one line. I defy you to find one line in the whole opinion where it says that the approach for interpretation is the framers' intent. What you find instead in that opinion is a general look at history. It looks back 2400 years. It looks at the use of the word "person" in the Eighth and Fourth Amendments from 1790 and concludes that these Amendments seemingly use the term in a postnatal sense.

But the approach for the Supreme Court in case after case has been to focus on the meaning given by those who framed and submitted a constitutional Amendment in order to determine its legal significance. What did the people in 1864-1866 have in mind? What were their purposes? And I say to you, take a look at the pages of the *Congressional Globe*,[16] look at the works of the AMA in the way it tried to influence the nation's legislatures,[17] and it is impossible to claim that the life of the fetus was no part of their discussions. It is impossible to come away from this research with any other view than that they intended to prevent a human being in fact from ever again being treated as less than a human by law. Moreover, they were precisely aware of the unborn child and of what medical science, beginning in 1827, had discovered about the fetus.[18] The same people who wrote these Amendments had been made aware by the physicians of the time what the unborn child was and they sought to protect it. It is impossible to say that the Court really adhered to a most basic rule of construction in *Roe v. Wade* when it neglected to look for the framers' true intent.

MONTGOMERY:

Isn't it possible that under the Court's present philosophy the Justices did not see restating the intent of the framers as their obligation, but rather responding to the pressures of today's society in which women's liberation has become one of the foremost problems of the time? The Court may also have been responding to the societal forces of self-centrism as spoken of by Professor Zuckman. Isn't it plain from the fact that the Court wants to dispense with a fusty medical profession that seems to be hanging on to a Hippocratic oath in a kind of naive and fundamentalist fashion by trying to prove that it is only the product of Pythagoreanism? Don't we have a tension here between two philoso-

---

[16]*Congressional Globe*, 39th Congress, 1st session, 1089 and 2766 (1866).
[17]Robert Byrn, "An American Tragedy: The Supreme Court on Abortion," *Fordham Law Review* XLI (1972-73), 835-38.
[18]Andre Hellegers, M.D., quoted in *Catholic News*, March 15, 1973, p. 11.

phies of constitutional interpretation? One school of thought is willing to alter the constitutional base of our government under the guise of ''interpretation,'' while the other school insists that a constitutional Amendment be labeled as such and only put into effect after the accepted mode of adoption has been completed.

DeMarce:

I would like to comment in relation to the sociological pressure, particularly that coming from the women's liberation movement. The problem here, as I see it and as I argued myself at the national convention of the Women's Equity Action League when they adopted a proabortion platform, is that ultimately by agreeing to a position in favor of abortion, women are undermining the entire moral and philosophical principle of the women's liberation movement. Women have been arguing for the past ten years that the fact that over the course of time men have accumulated positions of power is no reason for men to limit women's chances for employment or education. The men have no right just because they have the power. On the other hand, if women then turn around and say, ''we have the right to secure to ourselves an advantage at the expense of another category of human being—the unborn child,'' you are right back at a complete ''might makes right'' position. You are also saying by implication that if the power gives *us* the right, then anyone else has the right to try absolutely anything they are powerful enough to get away with.

Edward Dammich:

Professor Zuckman, earlier you made a point of people living up to their contracts. In your opinion, who are parties to the marriage contract and what obligations do they have to live up to?

ZUCKMAN:

I suppose you are suggesting that there are three parties to the marriage contract: the prospective husband and wife and the state. I accept the idea that the state has some interest in the marital relationship. It is debatable how much an interest the state has. I find it difficult to visualize exactly how you would ask the state to live up to its interest in the marital relationship, other than to provide an ordered society in which it can flourish. As for the two spouses, I would advocate making them live up to the promises they make to each other with the caveat that they have a free choice as to the kind of promises made. And then, of course, we would have to take another look at the whole scheme of divorce if we ever allow the parties themselves to define the marriage contract and the status they are accepting by it.

DAMMICH:

I am interested in the standing problem that seems to arise. Does the state have a greater interest in the marriage contract than it has in a contract between a dealer and manufacturer of a certain make of cars? If both parties to the sales contract decide they don't want to go through with the contract, the state, though it has an interest in assuring that commercial transactions are confirmed and business runs smoothly, will not step in and say, "Well, I'm sorry, but you cannot agree to dissolve this contract." And when we talk about parties living up to the contract the other side of the coin is, what are the remedies for failure? What are the remedies when the state fails to live up to its obligations under the contract? It just seems one-sided for the state.

52

ZUCKMAN:

Well, perhaps the denial of dissolution if the parties fail to live up to their bargain is a remedy, or the willingness of the courts to allow damages for the breach of the marital contract. Now it may seem somewhat farfetched that by the very process in which the state operates on the attempt to gain a remedy, it is in a sense fulfilling its obligations to the contract and protecting its interests in the contract.

QUESTION:

Professor Witherspoon, could you indicate the activity you fore- see for the legislature at the federal level in granting fathers stand- ing in abortion cases?

WITHERSPOON:

I think a very biblical uphill battle would be presented. Actually what I was urging was a focus on convincing the private sector to perceive the opportunity which is there for us. The energies of the private sector would then be focused with a view to going to the state legislatures and to the federal legislature seeking to imple- ment, in both legislative areas, the perfection of a father's stand- ing right, citing the Thirteenth Amendment as authority. While Congress has the expressed right to implement the Thirteenth Amendment, we know from cited cases that state legislatures also have the right to implement the Thirteenth Amendment. And I would add that I think we have a very good chance for success in the courts. *Planned Parenthood v. Danforth,* [19] which has recently

[19]*Planned Parenthood of Central Missouri v. Danforth,* 392 F. Sup. 1362 (E.D. Mo. 1975), appeal pending before Supreme Court, No. 74-1151.

been cited, is a decision which gives a foundation for the protection of the father's rights in marriage. There is a discussion that was laid out by the court in the *Danforth* case in which the court said the father and his spouse have a right stemming from the marriage contract to keep the marriage intact for its purposes. And the father has an interest as father in the unborn child. This case also develops some other interests each spouse has running in favor of recognizing the father.

QUESTION:

Returning to the idea of the marriage being treated as a contract, I think that in general it has been the case in the past and also in our own American lives that the marriage contract is seen necessarily containing *sui generis* clauses. It has unique features. So as a matter of fact, although the courts can decide to break the legal bond of the marriage, that does not suffice to put the parties back in their original status. The courts all have provisions for the loss incurred by the parties: alimony and child protection. The court really cannot undo what was done. A relationship is set up in marriage that has caused it to be a *sui generis* contract in the law. Divorce does not really break up the result of the marriage; you have children here, some things the parties have worked for together—not just property, but personal things—the loss incurred by the wife by being taken out of the competitive situation for years. One of the things courts never really face is the consequences which are left hanging in the air, more or less. For instance, to have a divorce and remarry with the prospect of actually supporting two families is economically prohibitive for most Americans. Certainly to have a second divorce and remarry with the prospect of supporting three families is too much. Thus the state action in a divorce does not dissolve a marriage, but rather arranges for an acceptable method for continuing the relation. The events which occur in a marriage cannot be broken off by a divorce. Virginia DeMarce was quite correct in pointing out that historically the two families were coming together. Nuclear families were merely a subdivision here and not too important. In fact, over in Lutheran theology betrothal was regarded as the main event and the marriage was merely something for the family to celebrate afterwards.

QUESTION:

I'd like to address a question to Father Curran. If marriage is seen as the arch upon which society is constructed, what are the implications of this for state legislation in the light of your statement concerning the role and function of law in matters of morality?

CURRAN:

Let me respond to that question and to Father McHugh's earlier remarks. I was trying to point out that, in the light of the teaching proposed in the Declaration on Religious Freedom of the Second Vatican Council, the Roman Catholic Church should change its understanding of the role and function of law in matters of private morality. This document accepted the concept of limited constitutional government. The state is not the same as society as a whole, an important distinction which I would want to add to Dr. May's remarks. The function of the state is much more limited than the function of society. In the matter of private morality, the state must give as much freedom as possible to the individual and intervene only when it is required by the public order with its threefold content—an order of justice, an order of peace, and an order of morality. Since an order of justice forms part of the criterion of public order, there can and will be a prophetic aspect about law. I willingly acknowledge there is a teaching and prophetic aspect to law, but this is not the only aspect of law and cannot be absolutized. In addition, there is the need for an order of public morality, and here, I think, one can see the societal importance of the family and the need for the state and its laws to recognize the societal importance of the family. So that if one accepts the theory that the family is the arch or cornerstone of society, the state has a legitimate function in preserving and promoting the family through appropriate legislation regarding marriage and divorce.

QUESTION:

Professor Zuckman, you called for the possibility of counseling during the waiting period for a no-fault divorce. I wonder what you would recommend if one of the parties absolutely refused to take part in a counseling process?

ZUCKMAN:

It seems to me that after a fair and reasonable time, if one of the parties will not be counseled that fact may only be taken as evidence of the breakdown, and the divorce proceeding should continue. In my judgment, the waiting period ought not to exceed one year. When you go beyond a year, all the problems of the migratory divorce begin to creep back into the system, even if it is a nonfault system. There is nothing in our society that can be done to force a party to accept counseling. Oh, I suppose arrest on grounds of contempt is possible, but even so the objective is to get the party back in the counselor's office, not the jail. While I don't believe there is anything we can do to force counseling, there are ways to head off recalcitrance to some extent. The counseling service should be made as easily available as possible. Counseling should be the responsibility of all citizens, not just those involved in the divorce. Thus the counseling should be tax-supported. I think a greater number of people will take the opportunity to try to salvage their marriage if the counseling is free.

QUESTION:

What of the possibility of preparing young people to accept the idea of marital counseling before they get married? Don't you think that young people should be impressed with the fact that if they find themselves growing psychologically apart from their spouse or confronted with one of the other fairly common marital problems, they should consent to professional counseling? Also, an awareness of the types of problems that may occur should be helpful.

ZUCKMAN:

I would certainly agree with that. I read a report from a school in Ohio in which men and women students were paired together as quasi-married. The couples then participated in a sort of board game in which they were each given $200 a month play money to take care of typical household expenses. A daily spin of a wheel would determine what problem they would have to cope with on that day. It may seem artificial, but the students actually began thinking about the problems. I'm sure the game emphasizes the need for open communication and points out the value of counseling when communication fails. I think we can reduce the problems of marriage and divorce by adequate premarital counseling—which our schools have not done, but could do.

MONTGOMERY:

It seems to me that if you get a situation where one of the parties absolutely refuses counseling—and the thumbscrew can't very well be used—then you have clear evidence of irremedial breakdown. Indeed, this is one of the defining marks or tests of irremedial breakdown.

Let me reemphasize my position on the no-fault question. Perhaps on the matter of maintaining a no-fault along with the fault system, I didn't make myself entirely clear. I certainly am not in favor of mixing the two approaches in a single structure. A mélange could cause all the problems Professor Zuckman so well outlined. What I am advocating is two independent and parallel systems, perhaps not as separated as law and equity, but at least two distinct systems—as exist for example in Virginia. For many people, not necessarily only the ones committed to Christian revelation, a subsequent marriage may be psychologically possible only where one has been vindicated with reference to the collapse of the previous marriage. You are familiar with the Scottish verdict of "guilt not proven." That practice hasn't been followed very widely elsewhere, perhaps because living with a guilt-not-proven verdict for a lifetime is not entirely satisfactory. In law, as in life, the issue of fault often has to be faced. In a divorce, the no-fault motif may actually carry the wrong connotation for the people involved. As C. S. Lewis' "old Western Man," I agree that the needs of a secular pluralistic society ought to be dealt with in the most sensitive kind of fashion. I am not suggesting at all that what we should do is to create a less adequate approximation of the Christian system and force the poor person who isn't a Christian to accommodate to it. A realistic analysis of the marital institution of the secularist in our society *does* show that in many instances a no-fault system is the lesser of evils when compared with the deception and heartaches that have often accompanied the misuse of the fault system. But in correcting this I see no reason to close the door to the very real and equally vital *mea culpa* which characterizes so many divorces.

QUESTION:

But why should that be handled by the civil law?

MONTGOMERY:

Simply because the civil law doesn't happen to exist *sui generis* without relationship to ultimate principles. We can't allow these two realms to exist in total isolation from each other. The question is not *whether* to connect them, but *how* to connect them properly.

McHUGH:

As I see it, first of all we are dealing with a total revision of marriage and divorce laws in which the state proclaims its interests as supportive of marriage and family life. It proclaims its interest in enabling people to live up to the marriage commitment, and it gives tangible evidence of that concern by committing social resources to support the family. Secondly, the state says through its laws that divorce is an unhappy thing. We the people are unhappy. We suffer whenever a divorce takes place. But because the marriage relationship is so highly personal, the potential for making a mistake in assigning blame for the breakdown is too great. And indeed it's better for all concerned to avoid legally placed blame. It seems to me that no-fault divorce comes closest to placing the responsibility for the guilt at the level of conscience, where essentially it belongs primarily. No matter what the courts do, they cannot be sure that they have chosen the right one to blame. I'm afraid that people who need an affirmation of blame from the law are really trying to get the law to fulfill a deep human need that it is not capable of fulfilling as a social institution. I think these people probably have another underlying problem that would benefit from spiritual or psychological counseling.

MONTGOMERY:

I would cheerfully agree with you that in an ideal world questions of personal guilt should not have to be dealt with by way of the legal structures of society. Wouldn't it be nice if, for example, society could handle cases of murder without any question of the *mens rea*, without any question of guilty intent. Surely no one wants the children of the murderer to be tainted psychologically or socially by any guilt associated with a court verdict. Yet I think it is obvious by an analogy such as this that realistically we happen to be living in a fallen and messy world where people cannot always have their psychological and spiritual needs satisfied along the most ideal lines. If you observe the general history of Western law, you see that the judicial structure has often functioned as a means—sometimes virtually the only means—capable of imparting to society at large the meaning of guilt. Exclusive focus on no-fault divorce may well be one aspect of the unfortunate trend in secular jurisprudence to avoid dealing with questions of guilt at all—a manifestation of the movement to separate entirely the notion of legal responsibility from moral responsibility. Obviously, these two are not identical; the law of the land, the positive law, is not equivalent to divine standards. But if guilt becomes a category inappropriate to the law in matters such as this, then I think we do both believers and nonbelievers a great disservice: believers are given no opportunity to obtain God-honoring judicial judgments, and nonbelievers are not reminded (as they ought to be) of the revelational standards which should lie at the root of all positive law and to which their own lives ought to conform. In sum, we must not sit idly by while revelational content is excluded from our judicial system; we have a duty to be sensitive not only to the immediate "short-range" needs of the nonbelievers, but also to the "long-range" need to keep the ideological climate open to revelational values.

DeMarce:

I have a real problem with the idea of divorce counseling. If the counseling is going to take place in a publicly sponsored or court-sponsored situation, then it seems to me that a puzzling problem is to what level of tolerable marriage relationship the spouses are to be counseled. The problem becomes greater when account is taken of the fact that undoubtedly they will have gone into the marriage with different expectations of the relationship to be established, depending on their own religious and cultural background. For many years I have been entranced by a delightful letter in the correspondence of Martin Luther. He is writing to the widowed mother of one of his students at Wittenburg, breaking the news that her son has fallen in love with a local girl and they would dearly like her consent to get married.[20] He is arguing that she should give the consent, saying quite simply after all marriage is an honorable and useful vocation, an estate instituted by God for the mutual aid and companionship of the spouses, the procreation of children, and prevention of fornication. This is his total definition of marriage. To tell the truth, if you take that as the goal, most marriages could be counseled to a tolerable level, I suspect, if there were the slightest amount of good will on the part of both parties. But the question of marital breakdown comes from normal demands made on today's marriage in excess of Luther's definition. The difficult question is at what level of tolerance a couple must consider their marriage still workable.

MONTGOMERY:

That is a very good point. How much difficulty has arisen from the romantic overlay of the nineteenth century—today's movie-star overlay that I suppose now transfers to TV! As a result of this immature fiction, people develop expectations for marriage that are so unrealistic that they can doom the relationship from the outset. Here we come back to the question of marital values in general—back to Professor Zuckman's point at the end of his paper. Ultimately the divorce problem focuses on the very concept of the family and on the existence and retention of a meaningful concept of marriage. In the final analysis the issue is squarely this: how are you going to deal with the self-centrism

---

[20]Martin Luther, "To Ursula Schneidewein June 4, 1539," in Theodore G. Tappert, editor and translator, *Luther: Letters of Spiritual Counsel*, XVIII, *Library of Christian Classics* (Philadelphia: The Westminster Press, 1955), 287-88. See also "Questions of Marriage and Sex," *ibid.*, 258-94. Cf. also "Luther's Exposition of the Sixth Commandment," *Concordia Triglotta*, F. Bente and W. Dau, editors (St. Louis: Concordia, 1921), pp. 637-43.

that's causing the fragmentation of marriage and the family *per se*? We've been talking about divorce—how best to clean up the subsequent mess—and that's important, of course. But fundamentally the problem is self-centrism, and neither the law nor any ecclesiastical body is capable of extirpating that. If Scripture says anything, it says that a living relationship with Jesus Christ is the *only* way to change a man's heart so that he stops thinking of himself as occupying a central position and looks to the interests of others. I think that's the lesson that should arise, that floats up as it were, from Professor Zuckman's paper (though I doubt that he was thinking precisely in those terms!).

QUESTION:

I'm particularly interested in the physician's role in the abortion decision. I think Dr. Marcin said that the abortion decision is "inherently a medical decision." If the decision is made in a therapeutic relationship, is it possible for a physician to refuse the therapy? Can you conceive of a situation where a doctor would deny "therapy" to a patient who requests an abortion?

MARCIN:

If you find yourself in that position, it would probably be your responsibility to refer the patient to someone who could deal with it.

QUESTION:

But on what grounds could a doctor deny therapy?

MARCIN:

Let's say religious. If there were medical grounds against it, I think the patient should be referred for a second opinion.

QUESTION:

From your experience and observations as a physician, would you say the medical profession was comfortable with having this role cast on them?

MARCIN:

My impression from reading and talking about how physicians are dealing with the task is that the feelings are mixed. Nathanson, in his article, concluded from his experience with over 60,000 abortions that he had presided over 60,000 deaths. He resigned as director of his program. However, I think there are many other physicians who have no qualms about recommending an abortion.

QUESTION:

Dr. Marcin, I'd like to ask a slightly more scientific question. When a pregnant woman presents herself to you, how many patients are you confronted with?

MARCIN:

That would depend on your philosophy as to whether the fetus is a human life.

QUESTION:

Well then, if the pregnant woman presented herself to you with some vague abdominal complaint, you would have no difficulty ordering an intravenous paradigm, gastrointestinal X-ray series, gall bladder studies, and any other kind of radiology screening studies we could conceive of.

MARCIN:

Well, obviously not, because of the danger to the fetus.

QUESTION:

Oh, the fetus! So there is another patient there you are concerned about, and it has nothing to do with religion or philosophy. So doctors recommending abortions are taking a very schizophrenic attitude.

MARCIN:

Yes, that's right. My specialty as a pediatrician may color my thinking, but when I am presented with a pregnant woman I definitely have an interest in the fetus. Before I could submit a pregnant mother to all that radiation, I would discuss with her thoroughly the possible effects on the baby. Other physicians bring that question up to the pregnant woman.

QUESTION:

The point I was trying to make is that medically you and I know that when the pregnant woman presents herself to us for care, we have at a minimum two patients. We might select death for one of them if we are so inclined, but our own scientific data makes it undeniable that there are two.

The medical profession is adopting a schizophrenic posture when it goes along with abortions per se. That is, we know there is a second patient for whom we have no therapy in mind and for whom we are selecting death. Now, I think that is a very unhealthy position for our profession.

QUESTION:

My question is related to the earlier discussion about how to prepare for marriage so as to minimize the risk of an irremedial breakdown. As a priest, is there anything you can do as a practical matter to prevent a marriage you consider unwise or ill-advised?

MCHUGH:

One of the things I wish to make note of is that in terms of support for marriage and family life, there is an increasing effort around the country today in Catholic Church circles to provide special help and counseling for under-eighteen-year-old couples and couples with an existing pregnancy who are presenting themselves for marriage. As the divorce statistics show, this is the most crucial group because they generally do not have the degree of maturity necessary to make the marital decision or their decision is forced by the pregnancy. Granted, a system of this nature has its risks, but there are advantages, too. A priest can refuse to marry a couple who cannot give reasonable assurance that they are capable of fulfilling the marriage commitment. The priest is concerned with the ability to live marriage both as a partnership and as a community of faith in covenant relationship.

QUESTION:

In other words, if a couple came to you and said we do not believe in the Catholic Church's teaching on the indissolubility of marriage, but we want you to marry us, you would refuse to marry them?

MCHUGH:

I would say that in conscience I can't marry you.

DEAN O'KEEFE:

The discussion seems to be going two separate ways—no-fault divorce and abortion. Perhaps the self-centrism noted in Professor Zuckman's paper is a common underlying cause of both the marital problems and the unthinking acceptance of abortion as an appropriate solution to an untimely pregnancy.

QUESTION:

What is available today in terms of counseling for married couples? It would seem from what has been said that counseling does not begin until the parties are ready for a divorce anyhow. I believe that in Illinois free counseling is not available until after the divorce papers are filed. But even if the lawyer is willing to counsel the couple who come to him, what training or expertise do lawyers have in counseling?

ZUCKMAN:

Well, there are pastoral counseling services all over the United States. It's my understanding that ability to pay has something to do with fees. If people can't pay, they are not going to be turned away, which I think is comforting. One problem we may have is that too many lawyers do not know of the resources available to the community for counseling. When an individual comes to them initially, the attorney may have a glimmer of a thought, as unsophisticated as he may be with interpersonal relationships in the marriage, that maybe they ought to have counseling. But he may make a horrendous mistake by starting to process the papers for a divorce before the counseling. Or he may make an even worse mistake by trying to counsel the couple himself. Divorce lawyers and lawyers by and large are not competent counselors. They ought to have a clear list of the various local counseling services, be on a first name basis with at least one person in each of the major services, and refer his clients to them. The lawyer's services would be much more valuable to the client if handled this way, and a number of hasty divorces might be avoided.

# 3: AMERICAN MEDICAL ASSOCIATION SYMPOSIUM: WHEN DOES LIFE BEGIN?*

QUESTION

Much of the debate that has been provoked by the legalization of abortions in a number of states centers about the question: "When does life begin?" Judging from what I have heard and read, objective opinions on this complex question are not readily found.

*Dr. Montgomery was the Protestant authority chosen to respond to this question by the editors of the *Journal of the American Medical Association* in 1970. Here follows his answer, together with the others also requested by *JAMA*. In publishing the answers, the *JAMA* editors carefully noted: "The answers here published have been prepared by competent authorities. They do not, however, represent the opinions of any medical or other organization unless specifically so stated in the reply."

Specifically, would you define life as beginning (1) with the first cell that forms when sperm and egg meet, or (2) when the cell has demonstrated life with the first cell division, or (3) with the first heartbeat, or (4) when the first wave activity can be demonstrated on the electroencephalogram, or (5) at the first possible time when life can be sustained outside the uterus or (6) when? Would it be possible for the American Medical Association to help shed some light on one of the most sensitive problems confronting our contemporary society?

MD, Ohio

This question was referred to six consultants: a lawyer; Protestant, Catholic, and Jewish theologians; a behavioral scientist; and an obstetrician-gynecologist, whose discussions, respectively, are as follows:

DOUGLAS STRIPP, attorney at law, Kansas City, Mo.

In most legal systems, legal personality begins at live birth.[1] However, there are several important exceptions to this general rule, such as the law of property which grants to a fetus yet unborn a conditional legal personality. That is to say, if a fetus is subsequently born alive it may immediately receive a legacy, obtain an injunction, have a guardian, or even be an executor, even though it was, at the critical moment, *en ventre sa mère*.

Moreover, according to a steadily growing number of recent cases in the area of tort law, a fetus can maintain an action for the death of a parent while it is still in *utero*. It has also been recently held by several courts that an action can be maintained on behalf

---

[1]"The Unborn Plaintiff," *Michigan Law Review*, 63, 1965, p. 579.

of a child who was born deformed because of prenatal injuries negligently inflicted upon it; and that an action can be maintained against a tort-feasor if the child dies—regardless of whether the death occurred before or after birth. Depending therefore on the particular jurisdiction involved, if the law of torts is concerned, human life may begin as soon as the child is capable of living apart from its mother (viable). Moreover, as of early 1965 eight American courts when dealing with cases in tort law followed a biological approach and now hold that life begins at conception, thereby according legal personality to the zygote.[2]

In the area of criminal law there is yet another exception to the general statement that life begins at birth, in that our state laws customarily define homicide as the killing of a fetus after it is viable.

Finally, it should be understood that in addition to the fact that the law first asks for what purpose we wish to know when life begins, our legal system proceeds on an *ad hoc* basis. Consequently, we cannot positively say that a future ruling will follow an earlier decision.

JOHN WARWICK MONTGOMERY, Ph.D., D.Theol.

Human life can, of course, be arbitrarily "defined" to begin at any of the points mentioned. The ancient common law emphasis on "quickening" illustrates how arbitrary such definitions often are, and how pragmatic are the considerations giving rise to them (in this case, workable sanctions against socially harmful abortion).

The medical profession and the Christian religion, however,

[2]*Ibid.*, pp. 589-90.

71

are so fully committed to the irreducible dignity and worth of individual human life that neither can be satisfied with arbitrary or pragmatic definitions capable of investing the nonhuman with humanity or of lowering the genuinely human to subhuman status. Though variations in theological and medical judgment can certainly be observed historically on the question, it is remarkable how closely biblical teaching (Exodus 21:22-25) and scientific evidence today enter into accord on the absolute cruciality of egg-and-sperm union as the point of origin of individual human life, as discussed by Dr. Melville Vincent and myself in separate symposium papers for the Christian Medical Society.[3]

The force of such biblical passages as Psalm 51:5 and Luke 1:15, 41 is entirely consistent with current biological evidence as summarized, for example, by Jules Carles, director of research at France's National Center for Scientific Research (CNRS):

This first cell [formed by sperm-and-egg union] is already the embryo of an autonomous living being with individual hereditary patrimony, such that if we knew the nature of the spermatozoid and the chromosomes involved, we could already at that point predict the characteristics of the child, the future color of his hair, and the illnesses to which he would be subject. In his mother's womb, where he will grow, he will not accept everything she brings to him, but only that which is necessary to his existence: thereby he will realize his hereditary patrimony. In that first cell the profound dynamism and the precise direction of life appears. . . . In spite of its fragility and its immense needs, an autonomous and genuinely living being has come into existence. . . . It is rather surprising to see certain physicians speak here of "potential life" as if the fertilized egg began its real life when it nests in the uterus. Modern biology does not deny the importance of nidation, but it sees it only as a condition—indispensable, to be sure—for the *development* of

---

[3]See Walter O. Spitzer and Carlyle L. Saylor, editors, *Birth Control and the Christian* (Wheaton, Ill.: Tyndale House, 1969), pp. 86-89.

the embryo and the *continuation* of a life already in existence.[4]

REV. JAMES T. MCHUGH, United States Catholic Conference, Washington, D.C.

Roman Catholic moral teaching has traditionally held that human life begins when God infuses the soul, the distinguishing feature of human existence. Man's life and God-given destiny, then, are necessarily intertwined. From the first moments of his existence he is caught up into an ongoing personal relationship with his Creator, one that reaches fulfillment in final and eternal union.

In the past, various theories have been advanced as to when the soul is infused. Aquinas, working from inadequate biological evidence, posited forty to eighty days after fertilization. Although we have had no certain knowledge as to the precise moment that ensoulment takes place, theologians have always held that in practice the fetus must be accorded all the rights of the human person from the moment of conception.

In our day, the theologian relies more and more upon the scientist to provide accurate scientific information as the background for ethical reflection. In regard to the question at hand, some scientists would see conception, i.e., the beginning of human life, as a process that is only fully completed and verifiable at implantation. Geneticists would argue that at the moment of fertilization the genetic blueprint is set up for each human person, and all that follows is a natural consequence of this determined plan. The ethician has no revealed knowledge of when life begins or when ensoulment takes place, but he can reasonably rely on the scientific evidence. He can conclude that human life is an ongoing

[4]Jules Carles, *La fécondation*, 5th edition (Paris: Presses Universitaires de France, 1967), pp. 81-82.

73

process at least from implantation, and most probably from fertilization.

Roman Catholic teaching has always placed a high value on human life, coming as it does from the creative hand of God and the biological potentiality of man and woman. Life then is to be supported and maintained from its first moment of existence; and accepting our human inability to pinpoint precisely the moment of its beginning, the theologian chooses the safest course and assumes that human life is present from the time of fertilization, that is, with the first cell formation when sperm and egg are joined. Ethical questions concerning maternal health care, prenatal care of the fetus, and abortion are all founded on this presupposition.

RABBI DAVID GRAUBART, D.D., Ph.D., The Bet Din, Chicago

The question, "When does life begin?" as any other problem relating to life, when posed to a Jewish theologian, must be viewed from the vantage point of a tradition. In Judaism, this is Scripture as illumined by rabbinic literature.

The Bible makes reference to the status of a fetus in the following passage from Exodus (21:22, 23):

If men strive, and hurt a woman with child, so that her fruit depart from her, and yet no mischief follow: he shall be surely punished, according as the woman's husband will lay upon him; and he shall pay as the judges determine. And if any mischief follow, then thou shalt give life for life.

The death of the unborn child is punishable by fine only, because the unborn child is not considered a living person.

The text is further interpreted in the rabbinic literature, where we learn when life begins. We are told that when a woman is having difficulty in giving birth, it is permissible to "cut up the child inside her womb and take it out limb by limb." The commentaries further tell us that "as long as the child did not come out into the world it is not called a living being and it is, therefore, permissible to take its life in order to save the life of its mother."

It is clear from all the authorities in Judaism that the embryo is not considered a living being, and that "once the head has appeared, this being must not be touched, for we may not set aside one human life to save another." The fetus is considered "the loin of its mother," or *pars viscera matrum*.

According to Jewish sources, the period to be considered is three months after conception; prior to this period, life has not yet begun.

ANDIE L. KNUTSON, Ph.D., University of California, Berkeley

Philosophers and scientists tend to agree that human life, as all life, is continuous, being passed through the germ cells from person to person. When a specific human life begins, however, is a question of ethical belief rather than one of science. The answer to this question depends upon how one defines a human life, and on this we are no closer to agreement than were the Greeks.

The professional definitions employed for the purpose of vital statistics and death registration were developed in cooperation with the World Health Assembly in 1950. Nearly all states now require that stillbirths be registered when the criterion of twenty weeks or more of gestation is satisfied. Most states, in addition, employ the criteria of (1) heart action, (2) breathing, and (3) movement of voluntary muscles. Death registration identifies the stillborn as a human death, and accordingly requires that disposal of the body be in accord with state regulations as regards human burial or cremation.

Hospital rules and procedures, medical codes, and other regulations concerned with health practice must, at a minimum, employ state definitions regarding the beginning of a human life and require action in conformity to those definitions in professional practice. In some settings, definitions may be employed which define a human life as beginning at an earlier point than that defined by law.

Studies of health professionals reveal wide variations in their personal beliefs. For one group of 350 health professionals, about 50% say a new life is a human life by the end of the first trimester; 30% during the second or third trimester or at birth; and 20% at viable birth or later. These findings have recently been corroborated (A. L. Knutson, unpublished data). Religion and sex appear to be significant factors related to such beliefs; professional education and experience do not seem to contribute greatly to their formation. Most important, however, are beliefs about the definition of a human life, the acceptance and definition of the concept of a human soul, and the time of the infusion of the soul into the new life. Conflicts are found to exist between personal beliefs and legal and medical codes which require conformity in professional behavior. Such conflicts tend to be the sources of considerable personal difficulty and discomfort in the performance of responsibilities.

Publications which discuss some of the views of other professionals are listed in the footnotes.[5]

---

[5]See A. L. Knutson, "When Does a Human Life Begin? Viewpoints of Public Health Professionals," *American Journal of Public Health.* LVII (1967), 2163-77. Also, A. L. Knutson, "The Definition and Value of a New Human Life," *Social Science and Medicine.* I (1967), 7-29.

## When Does Life Begin?

LANDRUM B. SHETTLES, M.D., Columbia University, College of Physicians & Surgeons, New York

Concerning when life begins, a particular aggregate of hereditary tendencies (genes and chromosomes) is first assembled at the moment of fertilization when an ovum is invaded by a spermatozoon. This restores the normal number of required chromosomes, 46, for survival, growth, and reproduction of a new composite individual.

By this definition, a new composite individual is started at the moment of fertilization. However, to survive, this individual needs a very specialized environment for nine months, then extended care for an indefinite period. But from the moment of fertilization a new hereditary composite is formed which, under appropriate conditions, will grow into a recognizable personality. From the union of the germ cells, there is under normal development a living, definite going concern. To interrupt a pregnancy at any stage is like cutting the link of a chain; the chain is broken no matter where the link is cut. Naturally the earlier a pregnancy is interrupted, the less the physical, objective encounter.

# 4:  THE CHRISTIAN VIEW OF THE FETUS

## Introduction

A superficial glance at the subject of this paper may suggest
exactly that: superficiality. In the late twentieth century, is it
really possible that theologians are still engaged in the kind of
scholastic nit-picking that led St. Thomas,[1] following Aristotle,[2]
to assert that the male receives his "rational soul" forty days
after conception while the female has to wait eighty to ninety

---

[1]*Summa Theologica*, Pt. I, quest. 75, art. i; cf. quest. 76, art. iii ad 3; quest.
118, art. ii ad 2.
[2]*Hist. Anim.*, vii. 3.

days for hers? Does our topic imply a revival of theological interest in intrauterine movement, such as led Samuel Pepys to write in his diary: "Lady Castlemaine quickened at my Lord Gerard's at dinner"?[3]

The relation of "soul" to "fetus" is of crucial importance for the whole abortion issue. Is abortion morally wrong, and if so, *how* wrong? The answer to this question depends squarely on the nature of the unborn child. Is it in fact a person prior to attaining viability? In theological parlance, does it possess a soul? Is it a being destined for eternal life, or merely a physiological growth within the mother (analogous to a tumor)? On the basis of responses to these questions the Christian will decide whether or not abortion is murder, and whether under any circumstances it can be morally justified.

The complexity, rather than superficiality, of our task comes from the necessity of interrelating at least five disciplines. First we must discuss the nature of the "soul" (theology), then the nature of the "fetus" (medical science). The answers to basic questions in those areas will force us to pose the ontological riddle concerning the nature of "personhood" (philosophy). And, finally, we must face the pressing moral and societal problem as to whether abortion ought to be allowed (ethics and the law).

## What Is the Soul?

As a descriptive tool, Hegel's dialectic is not limited to history and economics. Most fields of endeavor manifest from time to time ideological trends that swing from one extreme (thesis) to

---

[3]Entry for January 1, 1662 or 1663.

another (antithesis). In medicine, for example, preventive tonsillectomy has been vehemently accepted at certain times ("yank 'em") and equally vehemently rejected at others ("forget 'em"). Theology is not immune from such trends, and the issue as to the nature of the soul is a good example demonstrating this.

The traditional, "orthodox" theology of the church, both Roman Catholic and Protestant, has maintained a trichotomistic (body, soul, spirit) or dichotomistic/dualistic (body, soul) view of man. In this conception, which has had definite historical alignments with "faculty psychology,"[4] the soul has generally been regarded as the separable and immortal part of man, as contrasted with his mortal body.

Protestant liberalism of the early twentieth century, which flowered on the soil of nineteenth-century philosophical idealism, likewise stressed man's "immortal soul" (but for humanistic, rather than for strictly theological, reasons). Thus, in the neo-orthodox reaction of liberalism (beginning in the 1920's), a powerful reaction to this entire mode of thinking entered the picture. In an effort to oppose the anthropocentrism of the liberals, and influenced by the salutary psychosomatic trend in the science and medicine of the time, neo-orthodox theologians and their compatriots in biblical studies (the so-called "biblical theology movement") argued for a totally monistic view of man. Undoubtedly the most influential product of this thinking in German has been the articles dealing with ψυχή, σῶμα, πνεῦμα, σάρξ, καρδία, etc. in Kittel's *Theologisches Wörterbuch zum Neuen Testament*, and in English the

[4]See Gardner Murphy, *Historical Introduction to Modern Psychology*, revised edition (New York: Harcourt, Brace, 1949), *passim*. This work is of particular interest because of Murphy's stature in this field of parapsychology (cf. his *Challenge of Psychical Research* [New York: Harper, 1961]).

slim volume *The Body,* by Bishop John A. T. Robinson (subsequently famous—or infamous—for his *Honest to God*). Here an attempt was made, conjointly with the emphasis in the biblical research of those decades, to distinguish as sharply as possible "Greek thinking" (supposedly foreign to the true biblical message) from genuine "Hebrew thought." One result was the rejection as a Greek import into Christian theology of the entire concept of a separable, immortal soul. Thus Robinson categorically regarded the antithesis of body and soul as "foreign to the Hebrew," described the "Greek" dualistic position as the "angel in a slot machine," and asserted: "Man does not *have* a body, he *is* a body. . . . The soul does not survive a man—it simply goes out, draining away with the blood."[5] In this view, the terms "body" and "soul" (as, indeed, such other expressions of biblical anthropology as "flesh," "spirit," "heart," and "will") do not designate separate ontological entities: they rather speak of the same "psycho-physical unity" from different angles. In recent years, this same position has been accepted and promoted by theological existentialists[6] and by a number of "new shape" Roman Catholic biblical scholars.[7]

Much can be said for this "holistic" understanding of man. The textual support for it in Scripture is powerful, and it has received qualified acceptance among conservative theologians.[8]

[5]John A. T. Robinson, *The Body: A Study in Pauline Theology,* "Studies in Biblical Theology," No. 5 (London: SCM Press, 1952), p. 14.

[6]See Rudolf Bultmann, *Theology of the New Testament,* Kendrick Grobel, translator, I (London: SCM Press, 1951), 190-259.

[7]See, for example, Claude Tresmontant, *Essai sur la pensée hébraïque* (Paris: Editions du Cerf, 1953), pp. 87-143. Tresmontant, significantly, has published an appreciation of the thought of Teilhard de Chardin.

[8]That this is no exaggeration may be seen by comparing the editorial notes at Genesis 1:26 and 1 Thessalonians 5:23 in *The Scofield Reference Bible*—and even the index references to them in the editions of 1917 and 1967 (1st edition: "Man, tripartite nature of"; 2nd edition: "Man, nature").

The term "soul" both in the Old Testament (שֶׁפֶשׁ) and in the New ( ψυχή ) frequently designates simply an entity that breathes and therefore has life; both men and animals are so described.[9] Occasionally, "soul" is applied in a simple enumeration of persons, obviously without any attempt to delineate a separable aspect of man.[10] The vital biblical theme of the resurrection of the body argues in the strongest terms, over against the σῶμα-σῆμα motif in Eastern thought and Greek mysticism, that man's restoration in Christ must be a total, psychosomatic renewal. Liberalism deserved to be severely criticized for maintaining that man, because of his alleged native virtue, possesses a natural immortality; Scripture makes the whole man totally dependent on God not only for his present, but also for his future life. And the excuses offered by dualism for depreciating the body (medieval monasticism and clerical celibacy) and avoiding dynamic involvement in the physical secular world (blue-law fundamentalism) warranted the most rigorous theological opposition.

Yet the "monists" must themselves be faulted for extremism. In their eagerness to make a legitimate point, they committed the all-too-common human error of misusing and ignoring evidence on the other side. James Barr, in his epochal and badly needed critique of the methods of the "biblical theology movement," has shown that both the contributors to Kittel's *Wörterbuch* and Robinson's *The Body* sadly misuse philological data in an effort to build a case for the "Hebrew theological mentality." Barr rightly slaps Robinson's attempt to obliterate distinctions between such New Testament terms as σῶμα and σάρξ (so as to achieve more "psycho-physical unity")—and the same judgment could

[9]Genesis 2:7; 1:20ff. (cf. Romans 13:1; Revelation 16:3); 9:12ff.; Ezekiel 47:9; Proverbs 12:10 (cf. Genesis 44:30).
[10]Acts 2:41; 7:14.

equally apply to σῶμα and ψυχή: "No one supposes that the two words are completely synonymous in Paul."[11] For Barr, Robinson manifests "a total neglect of linguistic semantics."[12] This point is well taken, for though there is much scriptural evidence in behalf of the holistic view, there are, at the same time, not only passages in which a "faculty" approach is taken to man's nature,[13] but—even more important—passages clearly showing that the soul can be separated from the body and that it is capable of existence after the body's dissolution.[14] In Scripture, all life (whether here or hereafter) depends squarely on the God who creates and redeems it;[15] but an unqualified monism and a denial of life in the intermediate state between physical death and the general resurrection lose biblical warrant. It is highly significant in this connection that the force of total biblical teaching has led the world's foremost specialist on Luther's pneumatology to affirm a "*dichotomisch (zweistufig)*" theological anthropology.[16] The biblical scholar—or the lay Christian, for that matter—must

[11]James Barr, *The Semantics of Biblical Language* (London: Oxford University Press, 1961), p. 37.

[12]*Ibid.*, p. 35.

[13]Deuteronomy 4:29; 26:16; 1 Kings 8:48; 2 Kings 23:25; Micah 7:1; Matthew 16:26; 22:37 (cf. Deuteronomy 6:5); Acts 4:32; Hebrews 4:12.

[14]Matthew 10:28; Revelation 6:9; 20:4.

[15]Léon-Dufour makes the vital point, on the basis of James 1:21 and 1 Peter 1:8, 9, that the "souls under the altar" (Revelation 6:9; 20:4) are there only by "*un appel à la résurrection, oeuvre de l'Esprit de vie, non d'une force immanente. Dans l'âme Dieu a déposé une semence d'éternité qui germera en son temps*"—Xavier Léon-Dufour, editor, "Ame," *Vocabulaire de Théologie Biblique* (Paris: Editions du Cerf, 1964), p. 29. Léon-Dufour, a French Jesuit, is, like Claude Tresmontant (see above, note 7), a representative of the post-Vatican II "new shape" Roman Catholic theology, with both its positive and its negative characteristics; see my *Ecumenicity, Evangelicals and Rome* (Grand Rapids, Mich.: Zondervan, 1969).

[16]Regin Prenter, "Anthropologie, IV, Dogmatisch," *Die Religion in Geschichte und Gegenwart*, I (3. Aufl.; Tübingen, 1957), 420-24. Prenter's work on Luther, *Spiritus Creator*, contains detailed discussions of biblical anthropology.

take into account *all* scriptural data in arriving at biblical teaching; as a faithful inductivist, he must not make his theories a procrustean bed into which some data are forced and from which others are selectively excluded.

But how can the "holistic" and the "dualistic" views be reconciled? If man is a body-soul unity, how can he continue to exist after the dissolution of his body? The best answer seems to be that during the intermediate state between death and the general resurrection, some kind of "clothing" is given to the soul, whose "nakedness" is an abnormal condition.[17] This "clothing" or "tabernacle" could with some legitimacy be called a body (if we mean by "body" no more than a "soul covering"), for the New Testament makes clear that in God's creative activity there are many kinds of bodies, terrestrial and celestial.[18] On the other hand, it is definitely not the physical body of earthly life, since this has decayed; in this sense, man's soul is most certainly separable from his body and can function in dualistic isolation from it. Assuredly this is not "normal": it is a temporary state, mitigated by temporary "clothing," and ending at the time of the general resurrection. But it cannot be ignored.

## The Fetus and Personhood

Our examination of the biblical concept of the soul brought us to

[17]See 2 Corinthians 5:1-10; Revelation 6:9-11. This point has been well developed by Oscar Cullmann in his influential book, *Immortalité de l'âme ou résurrection des morts?* (Neuchâtel and Paris: Delachaux & Niestlé, 1956); translated in *Immortality and Resurrection*, Krister Stendahl, translator (New York: Macmillan, 1965), pp. 9-53. It is too bad that Cullman made such an invidious comparison between "immortality" and "resurrection" in his work; much of the criticism his book received has been due to unfortunate semantic overtones for which he himself was unwittingly responsible.

[18]1 Corinthians 15:35-44.

the conclusion that it is intimately, though not absolutely, connected with the life of the physical body. In general, we may regard "soul" as a theological term for the "person"—who, though he exists without his earthly body after physical death, is "clothed" temporarily even in that condition. Evidently, then, to conceive of the "person" apart from any and every "body" is not a biblical mode of thought. So considerable is the importance of the earthly body that one thinks naturally of the intermediate "tabernacle" as having a close enough relation with it to maintain continuity of the total person.

The intimate connection of soul and body in Scripture establishes a predisposition against the idea of a divine "superadding" of the soul to an already existent body, but such a possibility cannot be excluded *a priori*, since, as we have seen, the soul and the physical body must be considered ontologically distinct. The question of a possible superaddition of the soul to the fetus requires a brief glance at the venerable conflict between the *creationists* and the *traducianists*.[19]

"Creationism," or (better) "concreationism," is a theological position held by Pelagius, Peter Lombard, St. Thomas, the Roman Catholic ordinary magisterium (though that Church has never given the position solemn definition), and by most Calvinists. This view affirms that God creates souls *ex nihilo* and supplies them to developing individuals at conception or during the intrauterine period.

Dissent has existed in the creationist camp in regard to the time when God supplies the soul to the developing person: Does this

---

[19]On the issue, see especially R. Lacroix, *L'origine de l'âme humaine* (Quebec, 1945); R. Boigelot, *L'homme et l'univers* (Bruxelles, 1946); C. Fabro, *L'anima* (Roma, 1955; with valuable bibliography); and P. Overhage and Karl Rahner, *Das Problem der Hominisation* (Freiburg i.Br., 1961).

occur at the moment of conception or at a later point? Though St. Thomas, as we have noted, held to the latter viewpoint, the pressure of modern embryological knowledge has pushed creationist theologians more and more to the view that the soul is supplied by God when conception itself occurs. When sperm and ovum unite and the two pronuclei fuse, a process commences, governed by the DNA molecular pattern, that fixes the new individual's characteristics—and this occurs prior to the first division of the zygote. The following argument by the director of research at France's Centre National de Recherche Scientifique is typical of the judgments which have influenced creationists to focus their attention on the moment of conception:

Cette [première] cullule est déjà le premier embryon d'un vivant autonome avec son patrimoine héréditaire bien à lui, tant et si bien que si l'on connaissait le spermatozoïde qui est venu et les chromosomes qui se sont rencontrés, on pourrait déjà prévoir le tempérament de cet enfant, la couleur future de ses cheveux et les maladies auxquelles il sera sujet. Dans la mère où il va croître et grandir, il prenda, non pas tout ce que celle-ci lui apportera, mais ce qui lui sera nécessaire: il réalisera son patrimoine héréditaire. En lui vient d'apparaître le dynamisme profond et l'orientation précise de la vie: un nouvel être est concu. (. . .) Malgré sa fragilité et ses immenses besoins, un être autonome et bien vivant, dont on peut désormais briser mais non pas modifier le destin biologique, entre dans l'existence. (. . .) Il est assez surprenant de voir certains médecins parler ici de vie potentielle comme si l'ovule fécondé commençait sa vie réelle lorsqu'il s'est fixé sur l'utérus. La biologie moderne ne nie pas l'importance de la nidation, mais elle y voit seulement une condition, évidemment indispensable, pour le développement de l'embryon et la continuation d'une vie qui existe déjà.[20]

But does not the phenomenon of identical twins demand a later

[20]Jules Carles, *La fécondation* (Paris: Presses Universitaires de France, 1967), pp. 81-82. For an English translation of this important passage, see chapter 3 of the present book, or chapter 5, note 8.

point for the introduction of the soul? Identical twins result—just as does the ordinary single individual—from the fertilization of one ovum by one spermatozoid; but splitting brings about *two* developing embryos with identical hereditary patterns.[21] Must not the soul therefore enter the picture at the point when the two individuals become truly distinct? And what can be done with the analogous conundrum posed by Ettinger?

*Experiment 4.* Applying biochemical or microsurgical techniques to a newly fertilized human ovum, we force it to divide and separate, thereby producing identical twins where the undisturbed cell would have developed as a single individual. (Similar experiments have been performed with animals.)

An ordinary individual should probably be said to originate at the "moment" of conception. At any rate, there does not seem to be any other suitable time—certainly not the time of birth, because a Caesarean operation would have produced a living individual as well; and choice of any other stage of development of the foetus would be quite arbitrary.

Our brief, coarse, physical interference has resulted in two lives, two individuals, where before there was one. In a sense, we have created one life. Or perhaps we have destroyed one life, and created two, since neither individual is quite the same as the original one would have been.[22]

A minority of Roman Catholic theologians—the most persuasive being Hudeczek—have seen such arguments as definitive support for St. Thomas' mediate animation theory. But a close examination of Hudeczek's case reveals that it stands or falls on

[21]*Ibid.*, pp. 86-90. See also Jean Rostand (of the Académie Francaise), *L'heredite humaine*, 7th edition (Paris: Presses Universitaires de France, 1966), pp. 9-11.

[22]Robert C. W. Ettinger, *The Prospect of Immortality* (Garden City, N.Y.: Doubleday, 1964), p. 132. I have discussed the central thesis of Ettinger's book in my article "Cyronics and Orthodoxy," *Christianity Today*, XII (May 10, 1968), 816.

the scholastic principle that the soul, as a "rational" or "spiritual" entity, must be indivisible (*simplex*).[23] Our study of the biblical data on the soul certainly established no such *a priori* principle, and on what other ground could such a principle be asserted definitively? Perhaps the soul is as divisible as is the fertilized egg! If the resultant identical twins show remarkable affinities in appearance, temperament, habits, etc., and if (as we have seen) Scripture sets forth an intimate soul-body relationship, perhaps one can as legitimately speak of "twin souls" as of twin bodies!

But as we have found ourselves imperceptibly moving back toward the motif of psycho-physical unity, we have in fact been approaching the domain of the theological traducianists. "Materialistic" traducianism holds either that parents generate from inanimate matter not only the body but also the soul of the child, or that the soul is actually contained in the sperm and conveyed by organic generation. More attractive by far has been "spiritual" traducianism, often called "generationism," which asserts that the soul of the child derives from the souls of the parents. Augustine, in opposing the Pelagians and in his insistence on man's total depravity, held to generationism,[24] as did Luther and most theologians influenced by him. The Roman Church, while not solemnly defining creationism (as we noted), has seen fit through its ordinary magisterium to condemn both forms of traducianism.[25]

The contemporary orthodox Protestant systematician Mueller is quite right to use the traducianist-creationist dispute as an exam-

---

[23]M. Hudeczek, *"De tempore animationis foetus humani secundum embryologiam hodiernam,"* *Angelicum* (Roma), XXIX (1952), 162-181 (especially 175).

[24]Augustine, *Epist.*, 166.8.25; 190.4.14-15.

[25]See P. B. T. Bilaniuk, "Creationism," *New Catholic Encyclopedia,* IV (New York: McGraw, 1967), 428-29; "Traducianism," *ibid.*, 230.

ple of an "open question"—a question "on which the Word of God is silent."[26] In a sense it is a pseudo-problem: a special case of the more general question as to whether the appearance of a new human individual is an act of direct or mediate creation by God. But the conflict is very instructive from the point of view of the abortion question, for we see how, whether more obviously as in traducianism or less obviously in creationism, the point of origin of the individual is pushed backwards in time. For the traducianist, it would be absurd to regard the individual as commencing later than conception, for even his soul derives from his parents. For most creationists, the moment of conception is the point when the soul is bestowed. Even those theologians who follow Aquinas in his mediate animation theory now argue from the case of identical twins, analysis of which leads directly to the original fertilized egg as supplying what will become the total and identical hereditary constellation of genes and chromosomes for both individuals. Moreover, the Roman Church has long condemned the viewpoint that if one grants that the soul is supplied subsequent to conception, abortion would not be murder. Pope Innocent XI, in a decree of 2 March 1679, condemned this position;[27] the encyclical *Casti Connubii* (1930) reinforced the Church's unqualified opposition to abortion; and more recently (3 October 1964), Paul VI, in reviewing the doctrine for a group from the New England Obstetrical and Gynecological Society,[28]

---

[26]J. Theodore Mueller, *Christian Dogmatics* (St. Louis: Concordia, 1934), p. 58.

[27]Condemned was the following proposition: *"Videtur probabile omnem foetum (quamdiu in utero est) carere anima rationali et tunc primum incipere eamdem habere, cum paritur: ac consequenter dicendum erit, in nullo abortu homicidum committi"* (Denzinger, *Enchiridion*, ¶1052).

[28]*Pope Speaks*, X, 1964, 1.

repeated Pius XII's condemnation of abortion (26 November 1951).[29]

But cannot the force of the embryological evidence be reduced simply by recourse to contemporary philosophical attempts at defining "personhood" functionally? Granted that from the moment of conception everything has been supplied to produce an individual, can it really be said to *be* an individual prior to, say, the onset of its brain functions, or its viability, or its manifestation of rational activity—in short, prior to its genuine *functioning* as a human being? Should we not, with Van Peursen, choose as our starting point "the whole man in his ordinary, day-to-day conduct, attitudes and decisions. These things are not accretions to the human being who exists in himself *qua* substance (body plus soul), but they are the indispensable essence or core of man, without which he would not be man at all"?[30] If this is the case, abortion could hardly be murder, for the fetus lacks this "indispensable essence or core of man." Glanville Williams suggests brain-functioning as the *point de départ:*

> The soul, after all, is frequently associated with the mind, and until the brain is formed there can be no mind. By placing electrodes on the maternal abdomen over the foetal head, electric potentials ("brain waves") are discernible in the seventh month, i.e., shortly before the time of viability. If one were to compromise by taking, say, the beginning of the seventh month as the beginning of legal protection for the

---

[29]*Discorsi e radio messagi di sua santità pio XII,* 13.415. By the papal bull *Apostolicae sedis* (12 October 1869), the canon law penalty of excommunication was levied against those persons responsible for procuring abortions of nonviable fetuses.

[30]C. A. Van Peursen, *Body, Soul, Spirit: A Survey of the Body-Mind Problem,* H. H. Hoskins, translator (from the Dutch) (London: Oxford University Press, 1966), p. 181 (cf. pp. 188, 193, 194).

foetus, it would practically eliminate the present social problem of abortion.[31]

The answer to this is twofold. First, even from a totally secular viewpoint, the "functionalist" definition of man will not wash. What functions will be regarded as *truly* human—as *sine quibus non* for genuine humanity? Movement? (But what about total paralysis?) Intelligence? (But what degree of it?) Personhood escapes all such definitional attempts, and the reason appears to be that personality is a transcendent affair: the subjective "I" can never be totally objectified without destroying it.[32] If this is true, then one can hardly look for the origin-point of personhood anywhere other than at the moment when all potentialities necessary for its functioning enter the picture: namely, at conception. To argue otherwise is to become caught inextricably in a maze which would deny true humanity to those who, through organic defect, are incapable of carrying out certain rational activities (e.g., some mental cases). The efforts of the Third Reich "eugenically" to eliminate such "nonhumans" should give us no little pause here. Can we say that when a human being on the operating table undergoes suspension of activity he ceases to be human? As long as the native potentiality to function as a human being exists, one must be treated as human and must have his human rights protected.[33] Though the newborn child does little at

[31]Glanville Williams, *The Sanctity of Life and the Criminal Law* (London: Faber & Faber, 1958), p. 210.

[32]See my treatment of the "irreducible I" in "The Theologian's Craft: A Discussion of Theory Formation and Theory Testing in Theology," *American Scientific Affiliation Journal*, XVIII (September 1966), 74; reprinted in *The Suicide of Christian Theology* (Minneapolis: Bethany, 1970), pp. 267-313.

[33]The legal practice of "ascription of rights" well illustrates this point (see especially the writings of H. L. A. Hart): though the fetus cannot defend himself in court (any more than an infant can), society ascribes genuine legal rights to him and seeks to uphold them.

the time to justify its humanity (except to make an immediate pest of itself), its potentiality to exercise a range of human functions later rightly causes the law to regard its wanton destruction as murder in the full sense; and the same may be said by simple extension for the nonviable fetus.

Theologically, the argument is even stronger. Man is not man because of what he does or accomplishes. He is man because God made him. Though the little child engages in only a limited range of human activities, Jesus used him as the model for the Kingdom[34]—evidently because, as one of the "weak things of the world . . . to confound the wise,"[35] he illustrates God's grace rather than human works-righteousness. Even the term βρέφος, "unborn child, embryo, infant," is employed in one of the parallel passages relating children to God's Kingdom.[36] The same expression appears in the statement that when Mary visited Elizabeth, the unborn John the Baptist "leaped for joy" in Elizabeth's womb and she was filled with the Holy Spirit.[37] Peter parallels the ideal Christian with a βρέφος, [38] and Paul takes satisfaction that from Timothy's infancy ( ἀπό βρέφους ) he had had contact with God's revelation.[39] Moreover, the Bible regards personal identity as beginning with conception, and one's involvement in the sinful human situation as commencing at that very point: "Behold, I [not "it"] was shapen in iniquity; and in sin did my mother conceive me [not "it"]."[40] For the biblical writers, personhood in the most genuine sense begins no later

[34]Matthew 19:13-15; Mark 10:13-16.
[35]1 Corinthians 1:27.
[36]Luke 18:15.
[37]Luke 1:41, 44.
[38]1 Peter 2:2.
[39]2 Timothy 3:15.
[40]Psalm 51:5.

93

than conception; subsequent human acts illustrate this person-hood, they do not create it. Man *does* because he *is* (not the reverse), and he *is* because God brought about his psycho-physical existence in the miracle of conception.

### Abortion in Light of the Christian Ethic

We have now reached the point where ethical judgment can be made on the abortion question. Four considerations warrant the strongest possible emphasis.

1. Abortion is in fact homicide, for it terminates a genuine human life. God's revealed moral law in Holy Scripture, with its high view of the sanctity of life, is an absolute, and therefore to cut off human existence is always an evil, regardless of changing circumstances or "situations."[41]

2. Nonetheless, it must be clearly seen that Christians have no business "legislating morality" in such a way that their non-Christian neighbors are forced to adhere to laws which create impossible stresses for them. The divorce laws in some countries and in some states of the United States are of such severity that many non-Christians who never contracted their marriage on a proper foundation are forced to greater sin in attempting to cir-cumvent the legislation against divorce. Abortion problems are often analogous: the individual has put himself or herself in a situation where abortion might conceivably be the lesser of evils. Still an evil, definitely, and the law of the land must unflinchingly say so; but the penalties could well reflect the ambiguity of the

[41]The most effective presentation of this viewpoint in all its aspects is, in this writer's judgment, *Le respect de la vie* (Paris: Beauchesne, 1963), by the eminent French medical scientist Paul Chauchard. Cf. also Rousas J. Rushdoony, "Abor-tion," *The Encyclopedia of Christianity*, I, Edwin H. Palmer, editor (Wilming-ton, Del.: National Foundation for Christian Education, 1964), 20-23.

sinner's condition. As the law recognizes gradations of homicide, it should look with some understanding on abortions where the lesser-of-evils principle unquestionably comes into play. Certainly there is some social difference between an abortion-homicide and the murder of a full member of society, whose life intermeshes with the lives of many others.[42] We are not here advocating legal laxity, but we are underscoring a fact often forgotten by Christians; namely, that the purpose of a human court of law is not identical with that of the Great Assize.

3. Christians must not, however, tolerate the fallacious argument that the establishment of legal abortion would *per se* constitute a lesser of evils by allegedly eliminating illegal abortion. A recent and careful study of ten years of legal abortion practice in Sweden reached the conclusion that "the frequency of illegal abortion has if anything increased,"[43] and recommended that "a more restrictive attitude should be adopted in the evaluation of the grounds for legal abortion."[44] The causes of legal abortion stem

[42]The following judgment is admittedly overdrawn, but is there not some truth in it? "In comparison with other cases of murder, a minimum of harm is done by it [abortion]. . . . The victim's mind is not sufficiently developed to enable it to suffer from the contemplation of approaching suffering or death. It is incapable of feeling fear or terror. Nor is its consciousness sufficiently developed to enable it to suffer pain in appreciable degree. Its loss leaves no gap in any family circle, deprives no children of their breadwinner or their mother, no human being of a friend, helper or companion. The crime diffuses no sense of insecurity. No one feels a whit less safe because the crime has been committed. It is a racial crime, purely and solely. Its ill effect is not on society as it is, but in striking at the provision of future citizens, to take the place of those who are growing old; and by whose loss in the course of nature, the community must dwindle and die out, unless it is replenished by the birth and upbringing of children"—Charles Mercier, *Crime and Insanity* (London: Home University Library, 1911), pp. 212-13.

[43]Per Arén, *On Legal Abortion in Sweden: Tentative Evaluation of Justification of Frequency During Last Decade* ("Acta Obstetrica et Gynecologica Scandinavica," XXXVII, Supp. 1; Lund, 1958), 62.

[44]*Ibid.*, p. 70.

from much deeper considerations than can be touched through legalizing such operations. As a Planned Parenthood Federation conference on the subject recommended, sensing the underlying moral problems involved: "There should be encouragement . . . of higher standards of sexual conduct and of a greater sense of responsibility toward pregnancy."[45]

4. The lesser-of-evils principle referred to above can (and frequently does) apply to Christian ethical decisions in abortion cases. The Christian, no less than the non-Christian, lives in an ambiguous and sinful world, where few decisions can be regarded as unqualifiedly good—untainted by evil consequences. Thus the Christian physician may be called on to sacrifice the fetus for the mother, or the mother for the fetus. Decisions in cases like this will be agonizing, but there is no *a priori* way of knowing what to do. Given the particular medical problem, the Christian doctor will endeavor with all his skill to cheat the grim reaper to the maximum and bring the greatest good possible out of the given ambiguity.[46] And the Protestant, unlike his Roman Catholic *confrère,* will not casuistically endeavor to "justify" himself

---

[45]Mary S. Calderone, editor, *Abortion in the United States* (New York: Hoeber-Harper, 1958), p. 183.

[46]It is perhaps well to note that even for Protestant Christians (such as this writer) who are members of communions where infant baptism holds a place of great theological importance, the baptism issue does not automatically place the unborn child's welfare above the mother's. No possible interpretation of Scripture can yield the belief that children who die without baptism are *ipso facto* consigned to Hell or into a "limbo" state, and even the most "orthodox" of Lutheran theologians (e.g., Martin Chemnitz) made this perfectly clear; the destiny of such a child, though beyond human ken (as is, note well, the specific destiny of every individual, old or young—Matthew 25:31-46), rests in the hands of the Father of all mercies. As Augustine and Luther rightly maintained: *Contemptus sacramenti damnat, non privatio.* Thus the Christian physician must not decide a question of physical life or death on the basis of the unknown quantity of a given individual's ultimate personal salvation. (Cf. Mueller, *Christian Dogmatics,* pp. 499-500.)

through his decisions. Though in particular instances the Protestant may well arrive at the very same action as his Catholic counterpart, he will find his decisions—in which lesser evils still remain evils—driving him continually to the cross for forgiveness.[47] "Abortion" will suggest to him first and foremost the total human drama as well as his own life: an "arrested development" due to neglect of God's creative love—yet wondrously redeemable through the sacrifice of Christ for us all.

## Addendum

The reader of the preceding paper will have observed that its author has become convinced of the truly human character of the fetus, and that he has reached this conclusion on the basis both of medical and of theological considerations. The essayist therefore looks with particular severity on the practice of abortion, allowing it only in instances where abortion unquestionably constitutes the lesser of evils. This is in substance the viewpoint held by medical scientists such as Dr. M. O. Vincent, and theologians such as Helmut Thielecke:

> The fetus has its own autonomous life, which, despite all its reciprocal relationship to the maternal organism, is more than a mere part of this organism and possesses a certain independence. . . . These elementary biological facts should be sufficient to establish its status as a human being. . . . This makes it clear that here it is not a question—as it is in the case of contraception—whether a proffered gift can be responsibly accepted, but rather whether an already bestowed gift can be spurned, whether one dares to brush aside the arm of God after this arm has already been outstretched. Therefore here [in abortion] the order of crea-

---

[47]A point well made by George Forell in his writings on the Protestant social and individual ethic.

tion is infringed upon in a way that is completely different from that of the case of contraception.[48]

It would be less than fair to imply, however, that this "strong view" was universally represented by participants at the Evangelical Symposium on the Control of Human Reproduction held in Portsmouth, New Hampshire, in 1968. Some medical men (e.g., Drs. R. L. Willows and C. T. Reilly) and theologians (e.g., Drs. Bruce Waltke[49] and Kenneth Kantzer) have definite reservations as to the genuine humanity of the fetus and as to its possession of a human soul from the moment of conception. I shall not speak further in regard to the medical evidence bearing on this point, for I have already given a summary statement of what would appear to be the definitive considerations bearing on the question: the fact that the DNA molecular pattern, established at conception, is a package containing the entire hereditary makeup of the individual—the sum total of his characteristics as an independent individual (see above, the quotation from Jules Carles, corresponding to note 20). But an additional word is necessary in respect to a theological, or rather exegetical, argument introduced by Professor Waltke which strongly influenced the thinking of a number of Symposium participants (cf. the news report on the Symposium which appeared in *Christianity Today*, September 27, 1968, pp. 33, 34).

This argument, contained in Dr. Waltke's Symposium paper, regards Exodus 21:22-25 as definitive biblical proof that "in contrast to the mother, the fetus is not reckoned as a soul [*nephesh*]."

---

[48]Helmut Thielicke, *The Ethics of Sex*, John Doberstein, translator (New York: Harper, 1964), pp. 227-28.

[49]It is my understanding that in the years since the Symposium took place, Dr. Waltke has changed his view and would now agree with my position on the abortion issue.

But, wholly apart from specific exegetical considerations, one might raise the general hermeneutic question as to whether a statement of penalty in the legislation God gave to ancient Israel ought to establish the context of interpretation for the total biblical attitude to the value of the unborn child (including not only specific and nonphenomenological Old Testament assertions such as Psalm 51:5, but the general New Testament valuation of the βρέφος, as illustrated especially in Luke 1:41, 44). Should a passage such as Exodus 21 properly outweigh the analogy of the Incarnation itself, in which God became man at the moment when "conception by the Holy Ghost" occurred—not at a later time as the universally condemned and heretical adoptionists alleged? Do we not have in the very nature of Dr. Waltke's argument a common hermeneutical blunder: the erroneous perspective that does not properly distinguish law from gospel and that tends to view the New Testament in light of the Old, instead of the Old Covenant as comprehensible only in terms of the New?

Moreover, even on strictly exegetical grounds, Exodus 21:22-25 does not say what Dr. Waltke thinks it does. He follows the interpretation of David Mace[50] over against virtually all serious exegetes, classical and modern, in claiming that the passage distinguishes between a pregnant mother (whose life has to be compensated for by another life if killed) and her fetus (unworthy of such compensation). But Keil and Delitzsch,[51] after explaining that the passage demands *exactly* the same penalty for injuring the mother *or* the child ("but if injury occur [to the mother or the child], thou shalt give soul for soul, eye for eye, . . . wound for

<hr>

[50]David Mace, *Hebrew Marriage* (London: Epworth, 1953), note 6, p. 11.

[51]C. F. Keil and Franz Delitzsch, *Biblical Commentary on the Old Testament: The Pentateuch*, II, James Martin, translator (Grand Rapids, Mich.: Eerdmans, n.d.), 134-35.

wound''), comment in a lengthy note as to how the Septuagint translation of the Hebrew text has misled vernacular translators (and a few commentators like the Hellenizing Jew Philo) to adopt the view that

> the fruit, the premature birth of which was caused by the blow, if not yet developed into a human form, was not to be regarded as in any sense a human being, so that the giver of the blow was only required to pay a pecuniary compensation.[52]

But [continue Keil and Delitzsch] the arbitrary character of this explanation is apparent at once; for יֶלֶד only denotes a child, as a fully developed human being, and not the fruit of the womb before it has also assumed a human form. . . . The omission of לֹא , also, apparently renders it impracticable to refer the words to injury done to the woman alone.[53]

The full meaning of the passage is, then: "If men strove and thrust against a woman with child, who had come near or between them for the purpose of making peace, so that her children come out (come into the world), and no injury was done either to the woman or the child that was born, a pecuniary compensation was to be paid. . . . A fine is imposed, because even if no injury had been done to the woman and the fruit of her womb, such a blow might have endangered life."[54] But where injury occurred either to mother or unborn child (as we have noted), the *lex talionis* applied indiscriminately—to the genuinely human fetus as well as to his genuinely human parent.

This interpretation is presented not only by a classic Old Testament scholar such as the nineteenth-century Protestant Delitzsch, but equally by such contemporary Jewish exegetes as Cassuto,

[52]*Ibid.*
[53]*Ibid.*
[54]*Ibid.*

whose *Commentary on the Book of Exodus* is a landmark. Here are the relevant portions of Cassuto's explanatory rendering:

"When men strive together and they hurt unintentionally a woman with a child, and her children come forth but no mischief happens—that is, the woman and the children do not die—the one who hurt her shall surely be punished by a fine. But if any mischief happen, that is, if the woman dies or the children die, then you shall give life for life."[55]

To interpret the passage in any other way is to strain the text intolerably, and efforts at emendation (such as what S. R. Driver commended as Budde's "clever" suggestions) are neither necessary nor helpful. *The original text places a value on fetal life equal to that accorded to adult life, and in doing so perfectly conjoins with the rest of Holy Writ.*

[55]Umberto Cassuto, *Commentary on the Book of Exodus*, Israel Abrahams, translator (Jerusalem: Magnes Press, The Hebrew University, 1967), p. 275.

# 5: ABORTION AND THE LAW: THREE CLARIFICATIONS

"The unexamined life," declared Socrates, "is not worth living." Though this aphorism might seem to favor a proabortion view (since the unborn are in a poor position to examine their own *raison d'être*), we see it as a neutral heuristic principle: the more closely one examines the particulars of any legal issue, the more likely will light appear at the end of the tunnel (or womb). Our modest hope is to remove three misconceptions bearing on the legal aspects of the abortion question.

The method to be employed is a dangerous one: the jurisprudential examination of fundamentals. It was just such an approach that resulted in the firing of young attorney Littlefield from the prestigious firm of Bass and Marshall. Instead of a traditional brief citing cases, he had had the temerity to quote Cicero! "There were no cases cited from the Second Circuit at all. Sure, all the great jurisprudential scholars were there. Kant was there. Wittgenstein seemed to crop up. . . ." The immortal last words spoken to Littlefield by the partner to whom he submitted his work were: "Don't call this — a brief."[1] But whatever the present memorandum is called, it should at least aid those concerned with the legal aspects of abortion to think more clearly on the subject.

*Clarification One:* Roe v. Wade *Does Not Leave the Personhood of the Fetus as an Open Question*

Discussions of the current status of the abortion issue in American law frequently go on the assumption that change in abortion law in general and the revolution stemming from *Roe v. Wade* in particular do not require any ultimate decision as to whether the unborn are in fact "persons." This view is mightily reinforced by Mr. Justice Blackmun, speaking for the Court:

We need not resolve the difficult question of when life begins. When those trained in the respective disciplines of medicine, philosophy, and theology are unable to arrive at any consensus, the judiciary, at this point in the development of man's knowledge, is not in a position to speculate as to the answer.[2]

But the pragmatic results of the decision in *Roe v. Wade* have left little doubt in the minds of the general public, whether sophisticated or unsophisticated, that the personhood of the unborn

[1] J. J. Osborn, *The Associates* (Boston: Houghton Mifflin, 1979), pp. 212, 219.
[2] *Roe v. Wade*, 93 S. Ct. 705 (1973) at 730.

has undergone radical redefinition. One of California's most venerable and controversial trial lawyers, Vincent Hallinan, thus referred to *Roe v. Wade* in arguing another case shortly after that decision came down in 1973:

> Do you know who is the biggest dissenter, the most important dissenter, in the world at the moment? It is the United States Supreme Court, which, just a short while ago, came down and, ignoring Congress, legislators, biblical invocations, and religious groups, outlawed anti-abortion laws. "A woman," it said, "is the master of her own body and if at least for the first three months of pregnancy she doesn't want to have a child, that's up to her and her doctor, and no state and no nation has the right to restrict her in it." That, my friends, is a dissent from a policy that has existed for over four thousand years.[3]

A former law clerk of Associate Justice Powell quotes a typical letter Powell received after he had joined the seven-man majority in *Roe v. Wade:*

Dear Justice Powell,

My name is _____ and I am 15 years old—a sophomore in high school. . . .

I think it is wrong for a woman to have an abortion. Some people think it's not murder for someone to have an abortion, but I think it is. And when they make murdering helpless unborn children legal, how long will it be before it is legal to kill sick old people, the mentally retarded, etc.?

The Supreme Court, it seems to me, should be protecting the rights and lives of all people, not legalize the murder of the innocent people.

Please try to do whatever you can to help. Thank you for reading my letter.

Sincerely,

_____[4]

---

[3]Quoted in Norman Sheresky, *On Trial* (New York: Viking Press, 1977), p. 84.

[4]J. H. Wilkinson III, *Serving Justice* (New York: Charterhouse Books, 1974), p. 74.

Are these gut reactions wide of the mark? Did the Court manage an act of subtle alchemy in transmuting the fetus's right to life into the mother's right of privacy, while still leaving the personhood of the fetus an open question? We think not.

Blackmun's assertion that "we need not resolve the difficult question of when life begins" is belied by his references to the fetus as having "potential life."[5] Justice Stewart, in his concurring opinion, uses the descriptive phrase "potential future human life."[6] Clearly, human life is not synonymous with *potential* human life; an opposition is being created between actuality and potentiality—to the detriment of the fetus's personhood. The unborn, at least during the first trimester of pregnancy, is accorded no more than potential (not actual) personhood, and his rights are being correspondingly attenuated.

That this construction of *Roe v. Wade* is not overdrawn becomes especially plain when we note Blackmun's admission that

The appellee and certain *amici* argue that the fetus is a "person" within the language and meaning of the Fourteenth Amendment. In support of this, they outline at length and in detail the well-known facts of fetal development. If this suggestion of personhood is established, the appellant's case, of course, collapses, for the fetus's right to life is then guaranteed specifically by the Amendment. The appellant concedes as much on reargument.[7]

Thus the Court, by necessary implication, rejects the appellee's argument that the fetus is a person within the meaning of the Fourteenth Amendment. In doing so it *does*, for good or for ill, "resolve the difficult question of when life begins" (or, at least, as to when life does *not* begin)—the opinions of physicians,

[5]*Op. cit., Roe v. Wade*, at 725, 731.
[6]*Ibid.*, at 735.
[7]*Ibid.*, at 728.

philosophers, and theologians notwithstanding.

How could the Court arrive at its judgment, contrary as it is to "the well-known facts of fetal development"? How could it disregard the overwhelming evidence of contemporary genetics as to the personhood of the fetus?

This first cell [formed by sperm-and-egg union] is already the embryo of an autonomous living being with individual hereditary patrimony, such that if we knew the nature of the spermatozoid and the chromosomes involved, we could already at that point predict the characteristics of the child, the future color of his hair, and the illnesses to which he would be subject. In his mother's womb, where he will grow, he will not accept everything she brings to him, but only that which is necessary to his existence: thereby he will realize his hereditary patrimony. In that first cell the profound dynamism and the precise direction of life appears. . . . In spite of its fragility and its immense needs, an autonomous and genuinely living being has come into existence. . . . It is rather surprising to see certain physicians speak here of "potential life" as if the fertilized egg began its real life when it nests in the uterus. Modern biology does not deny the importance of nidation, but it sees it only as a condition—indispensable, to be sure—for the *development* of the embryo and the *continuation* of a life already in existence.[8]

Such hard data are ignored by the Court because the Court convinced itself that it was not in fact deciding the question of the fetus's personhood, and did not need to do so to arrive at its abortion decision. "The unexamined life is not worth living." By not examining what it was really doing, the Court uncritically and gratuitously deprived the unborn of personhood.

But would it not be fairer to the Court to say that when Blackmun states that "we need not resolve the difficult question of when life begins" he is merely declaring that the Court's task is

---

[8]Jules Carles, *La fécondation* (Paris: Presses Universitaires de France, 1967), pp. 81-82.

not to determine personhood in fact, but *legal* personhood? Is not the Court simply sticking to its legal task and refusing to enter into the medical or scientific realm?

Perhaps this was the Court's intention. Even if so, however, this will not rehabilitate *Roe v. Wade*; quite the contrary. For one must not create a legal definition of personhood which flies in the face of medical evidence as to what a person in fact is. In National Socialist law, the Jew—regardless of genetic evidence of his humanity—was deprived of his legal personhood and destroyed like worthless offal.[9] Prior to the American Civil War and the antislavery Amendments, such decisions as *Dred Scott* relegated slaves to the status of legal nonpersons in spite of clear biological evidence of their humanity.[10] Wherever legal personhood has been defined without reference to objective genetic criteria, the door has been opened to the most frightful consequences.

As in the tragic examples just mentioned, the majority in *Roe v. Wade* were influenced far more by social and policy considerations than by biological fact. "This holding," they say, "is consistent with the relative weights of the respective interests involved . . . and with the demands of the profound problems of the present day."[11] What problems? In particular, the impassioned demand of many women to be (in the previously quoted words of Hallinan) absolute "masters of their own bodies."[12] Only such essentially social considerations can explain the bi-

---

[9]Cf. J. W. Jones, *The Nazi Conception of Law* (New York: Oxford, 1939).
[10]*Dred Scott v. Sandford*, 19 Howard 393 (1857).
[11]*Op. cit., Roe v. Wade*, at 733.
[12]On the psycho-social dimensions of the abortion issue, see especially M. O. Vézina, *Journal d'une avortée* (Montreal: Editions La Presse, 1974); K. Luker, *Taking Chances: Abortion and the Decision Not to Contracept* (Berkeley, Calif.: University of California Press, 1976); L. B. Francke, *The Ambivalence of Abortion* (New York: Random House, 1978).

zarre reliance of the Court on Brandeis' 1890 "right to privacy" doctrine in a situation which bears virtually no relation to the original meaning of that legal principle.[13] (Would the Court now argue that whenever our privacy is potentially disturbed—e.g., by prying neighbors or obnoxious newsmen—we may kill the source of the disturbance and the result will be justifiable homicide?)

Into such a slough of despond did the Court stumble when it refused to face squarely the question as to when human life begins. It did not leave that essential question open; it closed it, to the untold detriment of the unborn. Perhaps, as in the *Dred Scott* case, nothing less than a constitutional Amendment will be required to rectify the muddy judicial thinking of the Court.

## *Clarification Two: The Recognition of the Unborn in Property and Inheritance Law Is of High Significance for the Abortion Issue*

It is generally conceded, even by those favoring the current relaxed standard of abortion, that in the area of property law Anglo-American jurisprudence has maintained remarkable concern for fetal rights.

In contrast to abortion and homicide, property law has long been one where the fetus at its earliest stages has been given recognition. Two cases decided in the late eighteenth century are representative of English common law. *Doe v. Clarke* held that an unborn child is one of the "children living" at the time of a testator's demise, and *Thellusson v. Woodford* enumerated fetal rights as including recovery, execution, de-

---

[13]Cf. M. L. Ernst and A. U. Schwartz, *Privacy* (New York: Macmillan, 1962); H. Gross, *Privacy—Its Legal Protection* (Dobbs Ferry, N.Y.: Oceana, 1964); G. D. Glenn, "Abortion and Inalienable Rights in Classical Liberalism," *American Journal of Jurisprudence* 20 (1975), 62-80.

vise and injunction. American courts were not hesitant to pick up the English common law, as evidenced by *Hall v. Hancock* in 1834 when it was held that a grandson born almost nine months after the testator's death was a beneficiary under a bequest to such grandchildren "as may be living at my death."

In America, *Crisfotd v. Starr* established the rule that an infant *en ventre sa mère* is deemed *in esse* for the purpose of taking an estate in remainder the same as if born. . . .

The Rule Against Perpetuities is perhaps the best instance of the *en ventre sa mère* doctrine coming into play. It is well established that a child *en ventre sa mère* is a life in being at the death of the testator. This effectuates an extension of the period recovered by the Rule to 21 years and period of gestation. . . .

In the area of trusts, the *en ventre sa mère* doctrine is just as firmly noted: upon the father's death, a child may be an income recipient of the father's trust before it is born.[14]

"Granted," is the usual response, "but all this means little or nothing, since where the right to life per se is at issue (homicide, etc.) protection has traditionally commenced only with 'quickening.' After all, we are dealing with a question of personhood; so property issues will perforce have little bearing."

This depreciation of the significance of property law for abortion discussion overlooks the place of property law in common law jurisprudence. In point of fact—as apologists for the socialist philosophy of law[15] and as American radical lawyers[16] have not

---

[14]Section III ("Property Law") of the essay, "The Commencement of Life: An Historical Review," forthcoming in the *Pepperdine University Law Review.*

[15]E.g., V. M. Chkhikvadze, editor, *The Soviet State and Law* (Moscow: Institute of State and Law, 1969).

[16]Cf. Jonathan Black, editor, *Radical Lawyers* (New York: Avon, 1971).

ceased to declare (with disgust)—traditional Anglo-American law elevates the concept of property to a sacral level.

Holdsworth speaks of "the most unique branch of the common law—the law of Real Property."[17] One of the ways in which that uniqueness manifested itself was in the high value placed upon property and the corresponding reticence of the courts or legislatures to tamper with existing property law. Writes Simpson in the concluding chapter of his standard *Introduction to the History of the Land Law:*

> Those who did understand the system encouraged the view that it was dangerous to meddle with so elaborate a structure, upon which the sacred property rights of the people were based. . . .

> . . . The old concepts of the law are not roughly handled; the definitions of Littleton and Coke still find their place in a modern textbook; lawyers can still gravely dispute the modern effects of *Quia Emptores.* For all the legislative interference which it has suffered, the law of property continues to display an extraordinary measure of historical continuity.[18]

Why do property rights carry a sacral quality in the common law? Let us hear from the two most influential writers of general legal textbooks in the history of the common law: Blackstone and Kent.

Blackstone, after discussing "The Rights of Persons" in Book I of his *Commentaries,* proceeds in Book II to treat "The Rights of Things." Book II, Chapter 1 deals with "Property in General," and there we read:

---

[17]W. Holdsworth, *A History of English Law,* II, 3rd edition (London: Methuen, 1923), 78.

[18]A. W. B. Simpson, *An Introduction to the History of the Land Law* (London: Oxford University Press, 1967), pp. 253, 261.

There is nothing which so generally strikes the imagination, and engages the affections of mankind, as the right of property; or that sole and despotic dominion which one man claims and exercises over the external things of the world, in total exclusion of the right of any other individual in the universe. . . .

In the beginning of the world, we were informed by holy writ, the all-bountiful Creator gave to man "dominion over all the earth; and over the fish of the sea, and over the fowl of the air, and over every living thing that moveth upon the earth." This is the only true and solid foundation of man's dominion over external things, whatever airy metaphysical notions may have been started by fanciful writers upon this subject. . . .

. . . In the case of habitations in particular, it was natural to observe that even the brute creation, to whom everything else was in common, maintained a kind of permanent property in their dwellings, especially for the protection of their young; that the birds of the air had nests, and the beasts of the field had caverns, the invasion of which they esteemed a very flagrant injustice, and would sacrifice their lives to preserve them. Hence a property was soon established in every man's house and homestall. . . .[19]

It will be noted that Blackstone unequivocally establishes property rights on a revelatory foundation, citing Genesis 1:28 and alluding to Jesus' words in Matthew 8:20 (parallel passage, Luke 9:58) as the source of his argument. For Blackstone, property law had divine sanction. Applying modern philosopher of religion Rudolf Otto's terminology, property in Blackstone's view was embraced in "the idea of the holy": it was sacral, an aspect of the *numen tremendens et fascinosum.*

Chancellor Kent, whose influence on American law in many

[19]W. Blackstone, *Commentaries,* 2-4.

ways corresponds to Blackstone's on English jurisprudence,[20] likewise sets forth a numinous conception of property rights.

> The sense of property is inherent in the human breast, and the gradual enlargement and cultivation of that sense, from its feeble force in the savage state, to its full vigor and maturity among polished nations, forms a very instructive portion of the history of civil society. Man was fitted and intended by the Author of his being for society and government, and for the acquisition and enjoyment of property. It is, to speak correctly, the law of his nature; and by obedience to this law, he brings all his faculties into exercise, and is enabled to display the various and exalted powers of the human mind.

> . . . The right of property, founded on occupancy, is suggested to the human mind by feeling and reason prior to the influence of positive institutions.[21]

Particularly illuminating is Kent's citation of authorities for his position. He quotes Selden's definition of natural law and refers to Aristotle, Plato, Cicero, and to Hooker's *Ecclesiastical Polity* in the same connection. On the principle of occupancy as establishing property rights, he quotes the fundamental aphorism from Justinian's *Digest*, *"Quod enim nullius est id ratione naturali occupanti conceditur"*;[22] the significance of this reference lies in the fact that Roman law distinguished between "civil" and "natural" acquisition of property, and classed acquisition by occupancy as "natural" (i.e., "recognized by the *jus*

---

[20]To be sure, one must never forget that Blackstone had the most profound effect on the education of American lawyers in the eighteenth and nineteenth centuries; see, e.g., J. S. Waterman, "Thomas Jefferson and Blackstone's Commentaries," in D. H. Flaherty, editor, *Essays in the History of Early American Law* (Chapel Hill, N.C.: University of North Carolina Press, 1969), pp. 451-88.

[21]J. Kent, *Commentaries*, 318-19.

[22]Justinian, *Digest*, 41.1.3.

*gentium*''[23]). Since the *jus gentium* is ''that law which natural reason has established among all men, is equally observed among all nations, and is called the 'law of nations,' as being the law which all nations use,''[24] Kent is saying that the root concepts of property ownership are part of the natural law deriving from no less a source than ''the Author of [man's] being.'' Thus the Chancellor, though during most of his life ''inclined to Unitarianism'' (as he put it)[25] and so more comfortable with arguments from natural law than from the Bible—Blackstone's ''holy writ''—held no less than Blackstone to a sacral view of property and of its concomitant legal relations.

Whatever may be the case in other legal systems, therefore, one cannot dichotomize person and property, to the detriment of the latter, in the context of the common law. Property, no less than personhood, is regarded as sacred—for both are part of the ''natural law'' and originate from the divine will.

Indeed, there is a sense in which property rights are superior to personal rights! Blackstone has already expressed his awe at ''the right of property . . . that sole and despotic dominion which one man claims and exercises over the external things of the world, in total exclusion of the right of any other individual in the universe.'' Here he alludes to the distinction between rights *in rem* as contrasted with rights *in personam:* whereas personal rights

---

[23]R. D. Melville, *A Manual of the Principles of Roman Law Relating to Persons, Property, and Obligations* (Edinburgh: W. Green, n.d.), pp. 213, 217.

[24]J. Black, *Black's Law Dictionary*, 4th edition (St. Paul, Minn.: West, 1957), p. 997.

[25]W. Kent, *Memoirs and Letters of James Kent* (Boston: Little, Brown and Co., 1898), p. 276. The Chancellor was, however, converted to evangelical Christianity before his death: ''Of late years my views have altered. I believe in the doctrines of the prayer books, as I understand them, and hope to be saved through the merits of Jesus Christ. . . . I rest my hopes of salvation on the Lord Jesus Christ'' (*ibid.*, pp. 276-77).

(rights in contract, etc.) are available only against some particular or determinate person or persons, rights *in rem* are available against the whole world. Digby observes that "the law dealing with rights *in rem* may be called—using the term 'property' in a large sense—the law of property, or the law dealing with property rights."

The rights and their corresponding duties which form the matter of English private law are first to be divided into two great classes, differing from each other in respect of the persons on whom the duties, which correlate to the rights, are incumbent. A person may have a right the essence of which consists in the fact that *all* other persons whatsoever are under a duty corresponding to the right; or he may have a right the essence of which consists in the fact that the corresponding duty is incumbent on some one or more *determinate* person or persons. An example of the first class of rights is the right of property which a person has in or over a piece of land or a herd of cattle. *All* other persons whatsoever are bound to abstain from acts injurious to his power of dealing as he pleases with his own. In other words, he may enjoy, use, and, if he pleases, if the thing is perishable, use up, the thing which is the subject of the right, subject only to certain general limitations, and also to certain special limitations prevailing in particular cases, where his rights are limited by conflicting rights possessed by other persons over the same subject. Rights of this class have received the name of rights *in rem*, an expression which means, *not* rights over things, but rights *available against all the world*, i.e., where a duty is incumbent on all persons whatsoever to abstain from acts injurious to the right.[26]

He continues, "If the word 'property' were not so ambiguous, one might venture to suggest that the 'law of property,' or 'of property rights,' should be substituted for the obscure expression 'rights *in rem*.' "

[26]K. E. Digby, *An Introduction to the History of the Law of Real Property with Original Authorities*, 4th edition (New York: Oxford, The Clarendon Press, 1892), pp. 298-300.

In other words, common-law jurisprudence imparts an absolute quality to property rights ("against all the world") which it hesitates to find in the realm of personal rights as such. We may of course disagree with such a jurisprudential philosophy, but we can hardly deny that this is what the common law is saying.

Nor can we deny the implications of this high view of property for the issue at hand; namely, the extent to which the common law regards the fetus as a person. In that realm of the common law—property rights—where the protections afforded are the most unqualified and absolute *(in rem)*, the fetus has most consistently been given recognition from the moment of conception. Putting it otherwise, when the common law has had its most unqualified rights at stake—inheritance, etc.—it has been the least willing to place the beginning of human life later than conception itself.

In light of this fundamental perspective of common-law jurisprudence, can we not agree with Byrn that the "quickening" issue is little more than a red herring?

Quickening was never intended as a substantive standard for the beginning of human life. It evolved purely as an evidentiary device. As a Massachusetts court observed in 1834: "The distinction between a woman being pregnant, and being quick with child, is applicable mainly, if not exclusively, to criminal cases" *(Hall v. Hancock).*[27]

In criminal cases, where the standard of proof has been very high (to a moral certainty, beyond reasonable doubt), it is understandable that evidentiary devices have been applied which give defendants the maximal benefit of the doubt. Quickening served as just such a device in an age of elementary medical knowledge.

[27]Robert M. Byrn, "Goodbye to the Judeo-Christian Era in Law." *America,* June 2, 1973, p. 512. *Hall v. Hancock* may be found in 32 Mass. (Pick.) 2-5, 26 A D 598 (1834).

Today, however, we have far more sophisticated techniques for determining the existence of life in the womb, and it is hopelessly anachronistic to stress the medieval quickening rule. Even more important, as we have been at pains to show, the history and spirit of the common law should lead us back from this byway to the main thoroughfare: that fundamental principle of *in rem* property law which declares that the rights of human beings are to be protected from the very moment of conception.

### Clarification Three: The International and Comparative Law of Human Rights Favors the Unborn

One often gets the impression by listening to advocates of the current relaxed view of abortion that *Roe v. Wade* finally brought the United States out of traditionalistic obscurantism into the modern world. We have already seen, however, that the Court arrived at its decision by totally ignoring current genetic knowledge as to the commencement of human life. Now let us face the equally unpleasant fact that our American case law now flies in the face not only of modern science, but also of the most recent and advanced developments in the international and comparative law of human rights.

It is true that some countries, such as France, have liberalized their abortion laws since *Roe v. Wade*.[28] But in the Federal Republic of Germany (BRD), the Federal Constitutional Court struck down the relaxed abortion provision of the Federal Diet's Fifth Law for the Reform of the Penal Code.[29] That decision now

[28]See J. H. Soutoul, *Conséquences d'une loi après 600 jours d'avortements légaux* (Paris: Table Ronde, 1977).

[29]Cf. H. O. J. Brown, "Abortion: Rights or Technalities? A Comparison of *Roe v. Wade* with the Abortion Decision of the German Federal Constitutional Court," *Human Life Review*, Summer 1975, pp. 60-85.

constitutes an admissible case before the European Commission of Human Rights.[30]

The overall picture of fetal rights in the international and comparative law of human rights has become clear through a landmark analysis by two French legal scholars, Alexandre Kiss and Jean-Bernard Marie.[31] They point out, *inter alia*, that even though it is true that the fetus does not automatically benefit from all the protections and freedoms afforded by international conventions, nevertheless, since the fetus is part of the mother's body, it "benefits by way of the mother from the protections accorded to her—specifically including the right to life" (example: Article 6 of the United Nations Covenant on Civil and Political Rights, prohibiting the execution of the death penalty pronounced against a pregnant woman; the same principle would apply *a fortiori* to torture and to cruel or inhuman treatment).

Moreover, the most recent international human rights agreements show increasing sensitivity to and concern for the protection of the human person from the very moment of conception. Thus the (nonobligatory) Declaration of the Rights of the Child states in its Preamble that the child "requires appropriate juridical protection before as well as after birth." The American Convention of Human Rights, which entered into force in 1978, declares (Article 4) that

Every person has the right to have his life respected. This right shall be protected by law and, in general, from the moment of conception. No one shall be arbitrarily deprived of his life.

The United States has not ratified the American Convention,

[30]*X. and Y. Against the Federal Republic of Germany.* Application No. 6959/74, decision of 19 May 1967 (19 *Yearbook*, pp. 382-416).

[31]Alexandre Kiss and Jean-Bernard Marie. "*Le droit à la vie: rapport juridique.*" *Human Rights* VII (1974), 338-53.

and the strong wording of this right-to-life article has worried more than a few congressmen: might not the United States, after ratification, find itself a defendant before the Inter-American Court of Human Rights because of *Roe v. Wade*?

Whether such a worry is realistic or not (and the U.S.—if it does ratify the Convention—may well take the coward's way out by qualifying its ratification of Article 4 by a "reservation" or "statement of understanding"), the American Convention sharply illustrates the tension between *Roe v. Wade* and the powerful trend toward maximizing human rights on the international scene. Just as there is a steady movement in municipal tort law toward giving a child wider legal opportunities to bring a cause of action to recover for negligently inflicted prenatal injuries[32]— just as in the realm of prenatal torts viability is less and less regarded as a meaningful criterion for recovery—so on the international plane the rights of the unborn are gaining ground continually.

One may therefore hope that scientific knowledge, jurisprudential self-analysis, and concern for human rights will finally bring contemporary American law to its senses in the matter of the protection of the lives of the unborn.[33]

[32]Cf. M. L. Closen and J. D. Wittenberg, "Recovery for Preconception Negligence," *Case & Comment*, September-October 1979, pp. 34-38.

[33]For additional jurisprudential analysis and critique of the current American abortion position, two readings are indispensable: R. A. Destro, "Abortion and the Constitution: The Need for a Life Protective Amendment," *California Law Review* LXIII (1975), p. 1250; and J. T. Noonan, *A Private Choice* (New York: Free Press, 1979).

# 6: ARE WE IN DANGER OF IMMINENT JUDGMENT?

There is a very real equality among sins. James tells us that "whosoever shall keep the whole law, and yet offend in one point, he is guilty of all."[1] In one of Charles Williams's novels, the descent into Hell of a specialist in military uniforms occurs when he commits the seemingly trivial sin of knowingly misleading others about the style of an epaulet. Since God's standards are no less than perfection, any sin can keep one from the Kingdom. Moreover, sins are equal in the sense that "the blood of Jesus Christ . . . cleanseth us from all sin."[2] No sin—except for

[1] James 2:10.
[2] 1 John 1:7.

121

the unpardonable sin of refusing redemption—is too heinous for Christ's redemptive cleansing at the last day.

Yet one can legitimately paraphrase George Orwell: while all sins are equal, some sins are more equal than others. That is to say, whereas all sins receive their just recompense at the last judgment, some sins are such an affront to the divine majesty that they are very likely also to trigger imminent judgment in the course of human history itself. In the Old Testament, for example, we read that one Uzzah was struck down on the spot for touching the Ark of the Covenant,[3] and the deaths of Ananias and Sapphira for attempting to deceive in spiritual things[4] is a not dissimilar New Testament incident. To be sure, God's ways are not our ways, and no one can presumptively say that certain sins will always be followed by imminent consequences; yet, at the same time, it would appear that there are some acts which by their very nature kindle the divine wrath and are likely to lead to immediate retribution.

One thinks of the destruction or perversion of marriage. The Bible presents the proper relationship between husband and wife as the highest analogy of the relationship between Christ and the church,[5] and frequently parallels apostasy and harlotry.[6] Thus, it does not seem unreasonable when the early church fathers so often argue that the collapse of marital standards among the Romans (as displayed, for example, in Petronius Arbiter's *Satyricon*) was a source of the divine judgment that led to Rome's fall. The fragility of the short-lived French Revolutionary governments—and their replacement by Napoleonic autocracy—was

[3]2 Samuel 6:6, 7.
[4]Acts 5.
[5]Ephesians 5.
[6]Hosea 1, 2.

due, at least in part, to the loose morals of the revolutionaries: one out of every five Parisian marriages ended in divorce in 1799-1800, and the nation could not survive the shock waves.[7]

The destruction of God's chosen people is another, even more obvious example. From the standpoint of eternity, it is not going too far to hypothesize that Hitler's "Thousand Year Reich" collapsed into a seething inferno in a single generation largely because the Führer and his cohorts attempted to exterminate the apple of God's eye—the people he chose as the vehicles of human salvation.

May I suggest a third area of potential imminent judgment? Each of the gross sins just mentioned ties by high analogy or direct interconnection with the essence of the plan of salvation. "Little children," as Scripture speaks of them, fall into this same category. "Suffer the little children to come unto me," Jesus said, ". . . for of such is the kingdom of God."[8] Destruction by the horror of being thrown into the sea with a millstone around the neck is associated with Babylon[9] and with those who do harm to little children.[10] A little child—unable to save himself and fully dependent—is, like the Jewish people, one of those "weak things of the world" chosen by God to "confound the wise."[11] Those who harm them do so at their peril, both in time and in eternity.

The early church was especially concerned with the interests of little children. In contrast with the callous and fatal exposure of unwanted infants by "cultured" Greeks and Romans, the

---

[7]Cf. J. M. Thompson, *Napoleon Bonaparte* (New York: Oxford, 1952), p. 181.
[8]Mark 10:14.
[9]Revelation 18:21.
[10]Matthew 18:1-6.
[11]1 Corinthians 1:27.

early Christians as a matter of conscience saved the lives of abandoned children.[12]

Since Scripture clearly teaches that the child's life begins at the moment of conception[13] and that he is a genuine person no less while in the womb than after birth,[14] early Christians likewise protected prenatal life and regarded abortion as homicide. In his apologetic against paganism, the second- and third-century Christian lawyer Minucius Felix declared: "I see your newly born sons exposed by you to wild beasts and birds of prey, or cruelly strangled to death. There are also women among you who, by taking certain drugs, destroy the beginnings of the future human being while it is still in the womb and are guilty of infanticide before they are mothers."[15] Such sentiments can be multiplied. Thus the anonymous Christian work, *The Prophetic Scriptures*, written before A.D. 325, asserts that "the embryo is a living thing" and that "abortive infants shall share the better fate," i.e., go to Heaven.[16]

The kairotic time has come for American Christians to bring this eschatological perspective to bear on our society. If God did not tolerate the Nazi extermination of six million Jews, what makes us think that he will continue to ignore our daily mounting toll of infanticides? I am not a prophet, nor the son of a prophet, but I see as less than accidental our simultaneous slaughter of the innocents and our declining domestic and foreign position. In baldest terms, the life we can save by a right-to-life Amendment to our federal Constitution may well be our own.

[12]See C. L. Brace, *Gesta Christi* (London: Hodder & Stoughton, 1886), chapter 7 ("Exposure of Children"); and especially E. Semichon, *Histoire des enfants abandonnes depuis l'antiquité jusqu' à nos jours* (Paris: E. Plon, 1880).
[13]Psalm 51:5.
[14]Luke 1:41, 44.
[15]Minucius Felix, *Octavius*, J. H. Freese, editor, XXX (1919), 82-83.
[16]Sections 48, 50.

# GENERAL INDEX

Abortion, 12, 13, 32, 36, 37, 38, 51, 53, 63ff., 80, 90, 94ff., chapter 5 *passim*, chapter 6 *passim;* legalized, 95
American Convention of Human Rights, 118, 119
Aquinas, Thomas, 19, 73, 79, 86, 87, 90
Aristotle, 79, 113
Augustine, 35, 89

Barr, James, 83, 84
Bernard, Dr. Jessie, 41
Birth control, chapter 1 *passim;* pill, 18, 20
Black, Justice, 49
Blackmun, Justice, 36, 47, 104, 106, 107
Blackstone, W., 111, 112, 113, 114
*Bolton*, 12, 13
Brunner, Emil 32

Calvinists, 86
Carles, Jules, 36, 72, 87, 98, 107
Cassuto, Umberto, 101
*Casti Connubii*, 18, 90
Chauchard, Paul, 21, 94
Conception, 36, 70, 71, 72. 73, 75, 77, 79, 86, 87, 88, 90, 91, 93, 94, 98, 107, 116, 117, 118, 124
Constitutional issues, 13, 32, 48, 49, 50, 51, 109, 124
Conversion, 34, 63
*Corpus Iuris Canonici*, 19
Creationism, 86-89
*Crisfotd v. Starr*, 110
Curran, Charles E., 42, 43, 55

Declaration of the Rights of the Child, 118
DeMarce, Virginia, 40, 42, 45, 51, 55, 61
Digby, K.E., 115

Divorce, 14, 33, 54, 55, 122, 123; law, 31, 32, 36, 39, 40, 41, 42, 44, 45, 46, 54, 56, 58, 59, 60; fault, 34, 35, 38, 39, 40, 58, 60; grounds for: adultery, 32, 34, 46, "irretrievable breakdown," 39, 40, 41, 46, 56, 58, 60, 62, 122; no-fault, 30, 31, 32, 34, 35, 38, 39, 40, 56, 58, 59, 60, 67
DNA, 87, 98
*Doe v. Israel*, 47, 48
*Doe v. Clarke*, 109
*Dred Scott*, 48, 108, 109

*Ethica Principia*, see *Moore, G. E.*
Ettinger, Robert C. W., 88
*Everson v. Board of Education*, 48, 49

"Faculty psychology," 81
Felix, Minucius, 124
Fertilization, see *conception*
Fetus, the, 12, 36, 50, 64ff., chapter 3 *passim*, chapter 4 *passim* (especially 85ff.; 97ff.), chapter 5 *passim*, 124
Fletcher, Joseph, 22
Fourteenth Amendment, 13, 49, 106
"Framers' intent," 49, 50

Graubart, Rabbi David, 74

Hallinan, Vincent, 105
*Hall v. Hancock*, 110, 116
Hegel, Georg Wilhelm Friedrich, 23, 80
Herod, 11, 12
Holdsworth, W., 111
Hudeczek, M., 88
Human rights, 117ff.

Justinian's *Digest*, 113

Keil, C. F. and Delitzsch, Franz, 99, 100
Kent, J., 111, 112, 113, 114
Kiss, Alexandre, 118

125

## General Index

Waltke, Dr. Bruce, 98, 99
Williams, Charles, 24, 121
Williams, Glanville, 91
Witherspoon, Joseph P., 12, 32, 47, 48, 53

Women's liberation movement, 50, 51

Zuckman, Harvey L., 30, 31, 34, 38, 41, 44, 46, 48, 52, 53, 56, 57, 58, 62, 67, 68

# SCRIPTURE INDEX